IMAGES OF W

AIRCRAFT CARRIERS OF THE UNITED STATES NAVY

RARE PHOTOGRAPHS FROM WARTIME ARCHIVES

Michael Green

Pen & Sword
MARITIME

First published in Great Britain in 2015
and reprinted in 2019, 2020 and 2021 by
PEN & SWORD MARITIME
An imprint of
Pen & Sword Books Ltd
47 Church Street
Barnsley
South Yorkshire
S70 2AS

DEDICATION

I would like to dedicate this book to Ivan F. Andes who served
on the USS *Saratoga* (CV-3) as a US navy gunnery officer
during the Second World War.

Copyright © Michael Green, 2015, **2019, 2020, 2021**

ISBN 978-1-78337-610-0

Typeset by Concept, Huddersfield, West Yorkshire HD4 5JL.
Printed and bound in England by CPI Group (UK) Ltd, Croydon CR0 4YY.

Pen & Sword Books Ltd incorporates the imprints of Pen & Sword Archaeology, Atlas, Aviation,
Battleground, Discovery, Family History, History, Maritime, Military, Naval, Politics, Railways, Select,
Social History, Transport, True Crime, and Claymore Press, Frontline Books, Leo Cooper,
Praetorian Press, Remember When, Seaforth Publishing and Wharncliffe.

For a complete list of Pen & Sword titles please contact
PEN & SWORD BOOKS LIMITED
47 Church Street, Barnsley, South Yorkshire, S70 2AS, England
E-mail: enquiries@pen-and-sword.co.uk
Website: www.pen-and-sword.co.uk

Contents

Foreword

To trace the history of United States navy aircraft carriers, it is essential to trace their history from the latter part of the First World War up until today. The American aircraft carrier grew up in uncertainty over its place in the fleet and uncertainty over the technology associated with this new type of ship and its fragile aircraft. As the technology matured and the US navy became more familiar and confident with carrier operations in the 1930s, the carrier took on an important role in the fleet. Nevertheless, this was a decidedly secondary role compared to the battleship, which was still seen as the ultimate arbiter of naval power.

The opening of the Second World War quickly upset this calculation. At a time when the US navy was still trying to figure out how to operate multiple carriers in a single formation and whether this was even desirable under wartime conditions, the Imperial Japanese Navy had created a revolution in naval warfare by combining all its fleet carriers into a single formation. The striking power of this unit was unsurpassed, and when combined with excellent aircraft and highly-trained air-crew, the Japanese began a rampage through the Pacific and Indian Oceans. The carrier was suddenly cast as the centrepiece of the US navy – a situation that remains unaltered today. Going into the Pacific theatre of operations, the US navy's carrier force certainly had its hands full as it learned how to fight a carrier war.

Fortunately for the US navy, it had spent considerable time during the pre-war era in mastering the basics of carrier operations. Going into the war, it possessed a number of large carriers and almost all of these saw action against the Japanese. The *Yorktown* class was a truly excellent design which demonstrated the US navy's emphasis on ships that could carry a large air group, thus giving the ship maximum offensive fighting power.

Built around the three *Yorktown*-class carriers, the Pacific Fleet was able to stem the Japanese tide in 1942 and take the first steps on the road to Tokyo. If the pre-war carriers stopped the Japanese, the flood of *Essex*-class carriers provided the muscle to push the Japanese all the way back to the Home Islands. This was the largest class of fleet carriers ever built and proved remarkably resilient and adaptable. So successful was this basic design that it was modified after the war, equipped with new innovations to allow it to operate jet-propelled aircraft, and saw extensive action during the first decades of the Cold War, including service in the Korean and Vietnam conflicts.

Not to be forgotten is the immense contributions of the smaller light aircraft carriers, and the unglamorous but essential escort carriers during the Second World

War. The escort carrier not only saw extensive service in the Pacific performing a variety of duties but also deployed in the Atlantic to take on the German U-boat menace. In 1943 alone, these ships helped to sink twenty-four U-boats and played a large role in turning the tide in the Atlantic campaign.

As the *Essex*-class carriers soldiered on into the Cold War, the first of the 'super-carriers', the *Forrestal* class, entered service in the 1950s. They were to be succeeded by progressively larger classes of supercarriers until the mid-1970s when the first of the *Nimitz*-class supercarriers were commissioned. These machines had over 100,000 tons full-load displacement and measured some 1,100 feet in length. The eighty-five or so aircraft carried aboard provided the US navy with the means to exert sea control against the growing threat of the Soviet navy and to project power ashore to almost anywhere on the planet. With nuclear power, the *Nimitz*-class carriers could easily stay on station anywhere in the world on a sustained basis and provide the backing not only to American military operations but often to American diplomacy.

All of this is well-covered in this single volume: from the first carrier which was nothing but a test platform converted from a collier and had no island, no hangar deck and little more than a flat deck to start the business of learning how to operate aircraft off ships. Up through to the carriers of today with their array of sophisticated technology permitting flight operations with the most modern aircraft in any kind of weather. Each of the ten *Nimitz*-class carriers operated by the US navy today has more aircraft embarked in a single hull than most nations have in their entire air force.

The strength of this work lies in the ability of the author to fully trace the development of the American carrier without getting bogged down in immense detail. The text is sharp and insightful and is supported by a well-chosen array of photography, giving the reader a full appreciation of the ships that have shaped US navy history over the last century.

Mark E. Stille
Commander, United States Navy (retired)

Acknowledgements

As with any published work, authors must depend on their friends for assistance. These include Michael Panchyshyn, fellow author Mark Stille, Peter Syvers and Orv Barr. The bulk of the historical photographs in this work were acquired from Real War Photos (operated by Jo Ellen and George D. Chizmar), the National Naval Aviation Museum and the National Archives. Some historical images were provided by Michael Pollock of Maritime Quest. More modern post-war images came from the United States Navy News Service and www.defenseimagery.mil, which is operated by the United States Department of Defense (DOD).

For brevity's sake the picture credits for Real War Photos will be shortened to 'RWP'. Those from the National Naval Aviation Museum will be abbreviated to 'NNAM' and the National Archives will appear as 'NA'. Images from the US Navy News Service and www.dimoc.mol will be credited to 'DOD' for the sake of brevity.

Chapter One

Pre-War Aircraft Carriers

The honour of designing and building the world's first true aircraft carrier goes to Great Britain's Royal Navy. An uncompleted Italian ocean liner was acquired from a British shipyard in September 1916 during the First World War and fitted with a continuous wooden flight deck 565 feet long, supported by a metal framework. The ship was named the HMS *Argus*. It was not commissioned (taken into official service) until September 1918, just as the war was coming to its end. However, the ship did much in the 1920s to help the Royal Navy work out the kinks in aircraft carrier design and operation.

US navy officers serving as observers with the Royal Navy during the First World War were very impressed with their efforts to come up with the world's first aircraft carrier, normally shortened to just 'carrier'. At the urging of these same officers, the US Navy Board organized hearings in the summer of 1918, attended by many of the leading aviators of the day. The opinions of these pilots were sought to assist in determining how much effort should be devoted by the US navy to having carriers of its own.

Upon the conclusion of the hearings in September 1918, it was recommended that six carriers be built within the next six years. These ships would have a flight deck 700 feet long, be capable of a maximum speed of 35 knots and have a cruising range of 10,000 miles. However, Josephus Daniels, the secretary of the US navy (an appointed civilian position), was not convinced that carriers were needed and quashed the plan in October 1918.

The First US Navy Carrier

Some in the US navy continued to push for the development of the carrier. In 1919 the US Congress authorized the conversion of a US navy collier into the country's first experimental carrier. Colliers were coal-hauling supply ships, employed by the navy from the late 1800s to the 1920s. There had originally been plans to convert a second collier into an experimental carrier but a 1922 arms control treaty agreed to by the US government put a stop to that project.

As the conversion of the collier into an experimental carrier began, the US navy decided to name it in honour of a very early American aviation pioneer, Samuel

Pierpont Langley. The experimental carrier was commissioned on 20 March 1922 and designated the USS *Langley* (CV-1). Unlike the more famous Wright brothers, Langley never managed to demonstrate a successful human-operated aircraft as the Wrights did in December 1903 at Kitty Hawk, North Carolina.

The prefix 'USS' stands for United States Ship and was instigated in 1907 when President Theodore Roosevelt signed an Executive Order to that effect. It has been applied to all the US navy carriers mentioned in this work. The letter suffix designation code 'CV' is the US navy's code for conventionally-powered aircraft carriers and is not an acronym, although there have been many variations over the decades such as CVE, CVL, CVB, CVA and CVN. The number/s following the suffix designation code for US navy carriers is a hull number for book-keeping purposes.

The USS *Langley* had an overall length of 542 feet. Unlike all US navy carriers that followed it into service, it did not have a hangar deck. Rather, its aircraft were stored in the ship's hold. When the time came to launch aircraft from the USS *Langley* they were brought up to the ship's main deck, located below the flight deck, by crane. Once the aircraft were on the main deck, they were prepped and then brought up to the flight deck by a single centreline elevator for launching. The wooden flight deck was held up by a metal framework.

In nautical terms, the 'main deck' of a ship is normally the highest complete deck (floor) extending from stem to stern and from side to side. The main deck is also typically considered a ship's 'strength deck'. A strength deck is a complete deck designed to carry not only deck loads but also hull stresses. On non-carrier ships the uppermost deck exposed to the elements is referred to as the 'weather deck' and if armoured is known as a 'protective deck'.

The planes launched from the USS *Langley* took off unassisted by mechanical means. They were assisted in take-off only by having the carrier sail into the wind to increase the amount of lift available for the aircraft's wings. For a brief time the *Langley*'s flight deck was fitted with two experimental compressed-air catapults to assist in the launching of the ship's aircraft. The ship was later fitted with a Norden mechanical flywheel-operated catapult.

Like HMS *Argus*, the USS *Langley* lacked any type of superstructure, commonly referred to as an 'island' on carriers, on its flight deck. HMS *Argus* had a small retractable wheelhouse that was raised from the flight deck when aircraft were not being launched or recovered. The navigation bridge extended out on either side of the *Argus*'s main deck. The navigation bridge is the station of the officer in charge of a ship.

The USS *Langley* had a navigation bridge at the bow of the ship underneath the most forward portion of the flight deck that included the functions of a wheelhouse. Both the Royal Navy and the US navy quickly realized that this arrangement was far from optimum and on most of their subsequent carriers an island of varying size was fitted. Carrier islands provide the space for a navigation bridge, staff officer functions and a flight control centre that can oversee the launching and recovery of aircraft.

Service Use

From 1924 to 1936 the USS *Langley* served with the US navy's Pacific Fleet and continued to perfect its operational capabilities. Upon the launching of the first plane from the flight deck of the ship, US navy Rear Admiral William A. Moffett declared: 'The air fleet of an enemy will never get within striking distance of our coasts as long as our aircraft carriers are able to carry the preponderance of air power to sea.' Not a pilot himself, Moffett was nevertheless a key player in the early adoption of the carrier by the US navy and the rise of naval aviation within the service.

By 1936 the *Langley*'s usefulness as an experimental aircraft carrier had run its course and it was converted into a seaplane tender. It was attacked by Japanese aircraft on 27 February 1942 near the coast of Indonesia and badly damaged. Rather than have it fall into enemy hands, the ship was sunk by its escorting destroyers; a sad and inglorious end to the US navy's first carrier.

The Impact of the Washington Naval Treaty of 1922

In February 1922 the Washington Naval Treaty, which limited the numbers of ships that could be built or retained by the world's leading navies, was signed by government representatives of the United States, the United Kingdom, France, Italy and Japan in Washington D.C. The treaty was an attempt by the civilian politicians of the respective countries to rein in what they believed to be a ruinous naval arms race which they feared would bankrupt their countries and possibly lead to another world war.

As battleships and battle-cruisers were the barometer of naval power in the early 1920s, the Washington Naval Treaty focused most of its concern on the number and characteristics of such ships then in service and those planned for the future. Less attention was given to the development of carriers as they seemed to be far less of a threat to the world's balance of naval might.

In fact, the Washington Naval Treaty proved to be very generous in allowing the navies of the various signatories to either convert existing ships into carriers or build new carriers from the ground up. This aspect of the treaty acted as a very powerful stimulus to the evolutionary development of carriers. There were also follow-on naval arms control treaties to supplement the original 1922 treaty which was to expire in 1938.

The Next Generation of US Navy Carriers

The United States and Great Britain received authorization from the Washington Naval Treaty to operate up to 135,000 tons of standard displacement for its carriers.

Japan received authorization for 81,000 tons of standard displacement, while France and Italy were restricted to 60,000 tons.

In nautical terms, displacement is the weight of the water displaced by a ship; this weight being equal to the weight of the vessel. By the terms of the Washington Naval Treaty, the term 'standard displacement' refers to a ship fully crewed with all armament and ammunition, minus its fuel and reserve boiler water. The tons listed under the treaty were long tons (2,240lb per ton), rather than short tons (2,000lb per ton).

There was another built-in cap in the Washington Naval Treaty, mandating that no carrier could exceed 27,000 tons of standard displacement. However, an important last-minute provision added to the treaty allowed all the signatories to build two carriers apiece with a standard displacement of 33,000 tons each from existing capital ships (battleships or battle-cruisers).

The US navy decided to convert two uncompleted battle-cruisers, originally intended to be scrapped per treaty requirements, into carriers. There was some controversy within the US navy at the time, as some felt that it made more sense to build a larger number of smaller carriers rather than fewer larger ones.

The first of the large converted carriers was the USS *Saratoga* (CV-3), which was commissioned on 16 November 1927. It was followed a month later by the commissioning of the USS *Lexington* (CV-2) on 14 December 1927. These vessels were also referred to as 'battle' or 'fleet' aircraft carriers, although these terms were never official US navy definitions.

Lexington-Class Carriers

Officially, the USS *Lexington* and the USS *Saratoga* formed the *Lexington* class of carriers. The US navy assigns ships of similar type into classes as they tend to share the same operational capabilities. The US navy, like other navies, names each class of ships after the first ship authorized in that class. Hence, despite the USS *Saratoga* being the first ship in its class to be commissioned, it was still listed as number three as the USS *Lexington* had been authorized first.

Due to the armoured hulls inherited from the battle-cruiser design, the standard displacement of the two *Lexington*-class carriers came in at 36,000 tons, thereby exceeding the limit set by the Washington Naval Treaty. The US navy circumvented this problem by using a clause in the arms control treaty that allowed the modernization of existing ships with 3,000 tons of additional armour for protection from both aerial and underwater attack. Full load displacement of the *Lexington*-class carriers was 41,000 tons.

In the US navy, the term 'full load displacement' refers to that of a ship ready to sail into action with a complete load of fuel and reserve boiler water. As with the term 'standard displacement', full displacement is measured in long tons (2,240lb per ton) rather than short tons (2,000lb per ton).

The overall length of the Lexington-class carriers was 888 feet. Both had been fitted with a single Norden mechanical flywheel-operated catapult on their flight decks for the occasional launch of a heavier floatplane (seaplane). The wheeled aircraft of the day were light enough to take off from the flight decks of both carriers without assistance. The catapults were seldom employed and were removed from both Lexington-class carriers in the mid-1930s. During a 1944 refit, the USS Saratoga had two hydraulically-operated flight deck catapults installed due to the increased size and weight of the latest aircraft.

The two Lexington-class carriers were designed to carry 80 aircraft but at a pinch they could store as many as 120. Extra planes were stored on the ships by hanging them from attachment points fixed to the overhead girders of the hangar deck. Aircraft were transported between the flight deck and the hangar deck by a single forward centreline elevator on both carriers. There was also a smaller centreline stern elevator employed for moving objects other than aircraft between the hangar deck and the flight deck on both vessels.

The hangar deck on both Lexington-class carriers was completely enclosed by the hull of the ship, limiting the number of planes that could be stored within and forcing the bulk of the ship's aircraft to be permanently stored on the flight deck. However, as carrier aircraft became more durable, this was not the problem it had once been with earlier more fragile planes.

Another factor that made hangar space on US navy carriers less of an issue than with other navies was due to US navy Captain (later Admiral) Joseph M. Reeves, who in the 1930s developed the doctrine of keeping the majority of a carrier's aircraft on the flight deck so they could be launched as quickly as possible when a call for action was received.

Reeves' doctrine also called for the quick refuelling and rearming of recovered aircraft on a carrier's flight deck so they could be launched back into the air without ever being brought below to a hangar deck for these purposes. The hangar deck was reserved solely for aircraft maintenance and storage; the opposite practice of British and Japanese navy carriers at the time. This is one of the reasons that US navy carriers of the day had larger aircraft complements than their foreign counterparts who kept all their aircraft in the hangar deck when not being launched or recovered. In 1943 the Royal Navy decided to adopt the American policy and store its planes on the flight deck of their carriers.

Unlike the USS Langley that had a wooden flight deck supported by a metal framework, the two Lexington-class carriers had a non-armoured metal flight deck covered by wooden planking. The hangar deck on the two Lexington-class vessels was the main deck, or strength deck. The deck below the hangar deck was armoured and therefore became the protective deck.

The US navy originally preferred non-armoured flight decks for a number of reasons. First, it was believed that they would be easier to repair in case of combat damage. Second, they allowed the carriers to embark more aircraft: the paramount design requirement for US navy carriers at that time was getting as many planes as possible to sea in order to launch the largest potential air strike. Having the hanger deck as the protective deck reduced the support structure of the flight deck relative to that required for an armoured flight deck, therefore reducing the ship's dis-placement and lowering the ship's centre of gravity, improving stability. This design feature of non-armoured flight decks was seen on all subsequent US navy carrier classes, up to the wartime-authorized *Midway*-class carriers commissioned after the Second World War that had armoured flight decks.

Service Use

The USS *Lexington* was delivering US Marine Corps fighter planes to Midway Island in the Pacific when the Japanese attacked Pearl Harbor, Hawaii on 7 December 1941. On 8 May 1942 during the Battle of the Coral Sea it was heavily damaged by Japanese aircraft-delivered bombs and torpedoes. In a valiant effort, the ship's damage-control parties managed to quench all the fires started by the enemy attack. However, petrol vapours from leaking onboard aviation fuel tanks eventually ignited, causing two large explosions and new fires that could not be stopped. The USS *Lexington* was ordered abandoned and to prevent it from being captured by the enemy, it was scuttled by two torpedoes fired from an escorting US navy destroyer.

The USS *Saratoga* was off the west coast of the United States when the Japanese attacked Pearl Harbor.

While steaming off Pearl Harbor on 11 January 1942 the USS *Saratoga* was struck by a torpedo fired from a Japanese navy submarine and damaged. In August 1942 the ship played a key role in the Battle of the Eastern Solomons, its planes sinking a Japanese navy light aircraft carrier. Later that same month, the *Saratoga* was struck by and survived another submarine-launched torpedo. It would then go on to serve alongside the Royal Navy in the Indian Ocean for several months in early 1944.

In the middle of 1944 the USS *Saratoga* returned to the United States for a refit and spent the rest of the year as a training ship for night-fighter squadrons. It returned to combat in January 1945 in support of the American invasion of Iwo Jima as a dedicated platform for night-fighters.

The development of US navy carriers optimized to operate night-fighters reflected the growing dependence of Japanese aircraft, beginning in 1943, on attacking American ships during the hours of darkness. This came about due to the ever-growing effectiveness of US navy shipboard anti-aircraft defences and fighters which made it almost impossible for Japanese aircraft to successfully attack during daylight hours.

Royal Navy officers from the aircraft carrier HMS *Victorious* (R38) who had chance to observe the USS *Saratoga* during its time in service during the Second World War made a number of mostly favourable observations about the ship and its pilots and flight crews. Some of these are listed as follows:

- The United States over a long period of time has intensively trained for carrier operations, experiencing better weather and using carriers better suited to aircraft handling. This has resulted in perfection of flying drill to the optimum point.
- All the fighter pilots aboard the *Saratoga* were as good as the best British fighter pilots on the *Victorious*.
- The dive-bombing of the American squadrons is superb.
- US torpedo squadrons are not as highly-trained as the British, nor are their torpedoes as good.
- Although US reconnaissance operations are not up to British standard because of a lack of highly-trained observers, need for such observers is not as great because of the excellent visibility which prevails in most Pacific operating areas and, of course, newly-developed radio aids.
- Training in ideal weather conditions contributes greatly to the perfection in performance of carrier squadrons. After some training in the Solomons [islands] the incidence of deck accidents aboard the *Victorious* was reduced to 1.3 per cent for 614 landings in the month of July 1943.

The USS *Saratoga* was heavily damaged by aerial Japanese bombs and kamikazes in February 1945 and returned to the West Coast of the United States, where it spent the remainder of the war as a training ship. It was employed as a target ship in July 1946 during Operation CROSSROADS, which involved the detonation of two atomic bombs in the Pacific. The ship suffered only minor damage from the first atomic bomb (airburst) being set off but succumbed to the damage inflicted by the second bomb's underwater detonation and subsequently sank.

Smaller Aircraft Carriers

The US navy had 69,000 tons of standard displacement remaining under the 1922 Washington Naval Treaty for additional carrier construction following the commissioning of the two *Lexington*-class vessels. They decided at that point to go with smaller carriers, with a standard tonnage of 13,800 tons. To validate the concept, it was decided to make the first ship a test model before proceeding with the construction of additional small carriers.

The first such carrier was the USS *Ranger* (CV-4), commissioned in June 1934. Due to the last-minute addition of an island, not called for in the original flush-deck design, the ship actually came in with a standard displacement of 14,500 tons. It was the first ship in the US navy designed from the keel up as a carrier. The USS *Ranger* had a full load displacement of 20,500 tons.

The *Ranger* incorporated new design features that subsequently appeared on later US navy carriers. These included a gallery deck located below the flight deck but above the hangar deck and a semi-open hangar deck with large roll-up metal curtain doors that could be closed in inclement weather conditions. The ship had an overall length of 769 feet with a flight deck serviced by three elevators, one centreline and two offset to the starboard centreline.

As the flight deck on the USS *Ranger* was a separate structure built upon the armoured hangar deck, the hangar deck was the ship's main deck or strength deck. Like that on the two *Lexington*-class carriers, the flight deck of the *Ranger* was made of non-armoured metal covered with wooden planking.

The semi-open hangar deck design of the *Ranger* was important, as it was originally intended to install two Norden mechanical flywheel-operated catapults within the hangar deck so that scout/observation planes could take off transversely without disturbing the launching of the majority of the ship's aircraft. This semi-open design also provided the ventilation needed when warming up the engines on the scout/observation planes prior to launching. As events transpired, the *Ranger* never had the hangar deck catapults installed. A hydraulically-operated flight deck catapult was installed on the ship during a 1944 refit.

Pre-Second World War service use of the USS *Ranger* quickly demonstrated that in concept it was a design dead-end. It had sufficient space to carry a respectable number of aircraft – seventy-six upon commissioning – but too many short-cuts had been made to keep the ship within the desired displacement limitations. It lacked a sufficient amount of armour protection. To fit all of its machinery within its narrow hull, it was missing the internal subdivisions that made the larger *Lexington*-class aircraft carriers more survivable in case of torpedo strikes or contact with underwater mines. It was also slower than its two larger cousins and lacked their seaworthiness in rougher water, making it difficult for the *Ranger* to launch and recover aircraft except in calm seas.

Service Use

Reflecting the US navy's lack of confidence in the design of the *Ranger*, it spent most of its career in the Atlantic Ocean rather than the Pacific. The high point of the ship's career came during the Allied invasion of French North Africa in November 1942. During that operation it was the only US navy carrier present and its planes played an active part in the fighting. By late 1943 the US navy considered the *Ranger* obsolete and returned it to the United States where it spent the rest of its service life as a training ship until being sold for scrap in 1947.

Yorktown-Class Carriers

Even before the commissioning of the USS *Ranger* in 1934 the US navy had decided, based on positive experiences with the USS *Saratoga* and USS *Lexington*, that the minimum effective displacement of carriers had to be at least 20,000 standard tons. This allowed for a sufficient amount of armour to be incorporated into the ship's design, vital for survival in combat.

In early 1931 with two large fleet carriers already in service and another carrier, the *Ranger*, still under construction, the US navy had officially used 83,000 standard tons of the total carrier displacement authorized by the Washington Naval Treaty. (The USS *Langley* was classified as an experimental ship and so did not figure in the US navy's carrier tonnage limitations.) The US navy therefore requested authorization from Congress to build two new carriers, each with a standard displacement of 20,000 tons.

Congress agreed to the request and in 1933 authorized the construction of two more carriers: the USS *Yorktown* (CV-5) and the USS *Enterprise* (CV-6). The USS *Yorktown* was commissioned in 1937 and the USS *Enterprise* the following year. These two new ships comprised the *Yorktown* class of carriers. They came in with a standard displacement of 19,900 tons and their full load displacement was 25,500 tons.

As the USS *Ranger* represented state-of-the-art carrier design when built, some of its design features were carried over into the *Yorktown*-class carriers. These included the semi-open hangar deck featuring the large roll-up metal curtain doors and a gallery deck located below the flight deck but above the hangar deck. For protection from aerial attack, the catwalks just below and around the flight deck of the *Yorktown* class were initially fitted with water-cooled .50 calibre machine guns, later replaced in wartime by air-cooled, Swiss-designed 20mm automatic cannons in single mounts.

The two *Yorktown*-class carriers had an overall length of 809 feet 6 inches. Their flight decks were serviced by three large centreline elevators, enhancing their ability to rapidly form up planes for combat. The ships were designed to operate 80 aircraft but had space for 120. They had two flight deck hydraulically-operated catapults and a single hydraulically-operated hangar deck catapult. Wartime experience showed that the hangar deck catapults were seldom employed and they were removed in 1942 as the separate scout/observation plane role was being taken over by dual-purpose aircraft.

Service Use

The USS *Yorktown* was in the Atlantic when the Japanese struck Pearl Harbor and was quickly ordered to the Pacific. The ship saw its first combat action against the Japanese early in 1942, conducting raids on Japanese forces.

During the May 1942 Battle of the Coral Sea an enemy bomb penetrated the *Yorktown*'s flight deck and exploded, killing and wounding many of the crew. Upon returning to Pearl Harbor for repairs, estimated to take at least three months, the ship underwent some temporary repairs instead and was placed back into service three days later, in time for the June 1942 Battle of Midway.

During the Battle of Midway the USS *Yorktown*'s aircraft damaged two Japanese carriers but in turn, Japanese carrier-launched aircraft successfully bombed and torpedoed the American carrier, which was eventually finished off by two torpedoes from the Japanese submarine *I-168* on 7 June 1942.

The USS *Enterprise* was delivering fighter planes to Wake Island in the Pacific when the Japanese attack at Pearl Harbor took place. Like its sister ship the USS *Yorktown*, USS *Enterprise* quickly went on the offensive in early 1942 in a series of raids on Japanese forces.

The *Enterprise* missed the Battle of the Coral Sea but played a crucial role during the Battle of Midway, with its aircraft responsible for sinking two Japanese carriers and damaging a third. The USS *Enterprise* suffered no damage during that famous naval battle.

In August 1942 during the Battle of the Eastern Solomons the USS *Enterprise* was struck by three bombs. After being repaired at Pearl Harbor, the ship took part in the Battle of the Santa Cruz Islands in October 1942 and was damaged by two enemy bombs. This time, repairs to the ship took place at Noumea, New Caledonia in the south-west Pacific. With repairs still in progress, the *Enterprise* played a part in the November 1942 naval Battle of Guadalcanal with its planes assisting in sinking a Japanese battleship.

Upon arrival at Pearl Harbor in May 1943, the USS *Enterprise* received the first Presidential Unit Citation presented to a US navy carrier. From Pearl Harbor, the ship returned to the United States for a badly-needed overhaul and modernization which began in July 1943.

One of the important updates to the *Enterprise* during its 1943 Stateside overhaul and modernization was the addition of more lower hull protection from torpedo attack, which had sunk its sister ship the USS *Yorktown* the year before. She also received numerous 40mm anti-aircraft guns. The added weight imposed by the beefed-up torpedo protection and AA guns pushed up the full load displacement of the ship to 32,060 tons.

Upon completion of its 1943 modernization programme, the USS *Enterprise* returned to the Pacific in November 1943. It went on to participate in many operations, the best-known being the June 1944 Battle of the Philippine Sea and the Battle of Leyte Gulf in October 1944. By December 1944 the *Enterprise* was equipped with night-operational aircraft.

The final wartime damage inflicted on the USS *Enterprise* occurred on 14 May 1945 when a Japanese kamikaze struck abaft the forward centreline elevator, killing fourteen men and wounding another thirty-four. It then returned to the West Coast of the United States for repairs and was there when the Second World War ended on 15 August 1945. The ship was decommissioned in February 1947. Plans to turn it into a museum ship failed and it was sold for scrap in July 1958, despite being the most decorated US navy ship in history.

Another Small Carrier

With its remaining standard tonnage displacement authorized under the Washington Naval Treaty, the US navy opted for the building of an additional small carrier, despite the poor experience it had had with the USS *Ranger*. This resulted in the construction of the USS *Wasp* (CV-7), commissioned in April 1940.

The standard displacement of the *Wasp* was 14,700 tons, with a full load displacement of 18,500 tons. It had an overall length of 769 feet and typically carried eighty aircraft. Planes on the ship were moved between the flight deck and the hangar deck by two centreline elevators. There was also a small deck-edge elevator added to the ship's design; its proven usefulness resulted in much larger versions being added to follow-on US navy carrier classes. The *Wasp* was fitted with two hydraulically-operated flight deck catapults and two hydraulically-operated hangar deck catapults.

Service Use

As with the USS *Ranger*, the US navy did not think very highly of the USS *Wasp*'s capabilities and restricted it during the early part of the Second World War to secondary theatres of operations such as the Mediterranean. By May 1942, as the intensity of combat operations in the Pacific increased and the US navy was down to only three fleet carriers, it was decided that the USS *Wasp*, despite its many limitations, had to be moved to the Pacific until more capable fleet carriers could be brought into service. The *Wasp* arrived too late to participate in the Battle of Midway but did see action during the initial phase of the American military invasion of Guadalcanal in August 1942, alongside the USS *Enterprise* and *Saratoga*.

On 15 September 1942 the USS *Wasp* was escorting a convoy of US Marine Corps infantry to Guadalcanal when the ship was spotted by a Japanese submarine that fired six torpedoes, three of which struck the carrier. The torpedo strikes caused massive aviation fuel fires that quickly engulfed it, in turn setting off ammunition fires. Despite the best efforts of the ship's damage-control parties, the USS *Wasp* was soon ordered abandoned. To prevent it falling into enemy hands, it was sunk by torpedoes from its escorting destroyers. Losses on the ship totalled 193 killed and 366 wounded.

One Last *Yorktown*-Class Carrier

With the Japanese withdrawal from the Washington Naval Treaty in 1934 and a subsequent naval build-up combined with the rise to power of the National Socialists in Germany beginning in 1933, the United States government became more mindful of the ever-growing danger that these warlike nations might pose to America. However, despite this awareness, the American government decided to wait for the Washington Naval Treaty to expire in 1938 before approving the building of additional carriers.

Under the Naval Expansion Act of 17 May 1938, Congress allowed the US navy an additional 40,000 tons of standard displacement for the construction of carriers. The navy wasted no time and ordered two carriers; one of these a third *Yorktown*-class carrier as that was the most modern design it then had in service and could be built in the shortest amount of time. The second carrier ordered was to be a larger improved version of the *Yorktown* class that would be known as the *Essex* class.

The third *Yorktown*-class carrier was the USS *Hornet* (CV-8). It was authorized in March 1939 and commissioned in October 1941. This was only weeks before the Japanese attack on the US navy base at Pearl Harbor, Hawaii on 7 December 1941, making it the last US navy carrier built within the Washington Naval Treaty limits. It did feature some design improvements over its two main predecessors, with the major external differences seen in the appearance of the ship's island.

Service Use

The USS *Hornet* was undergoing training activities off the East Coast of the United States when the Japanese attack at Pearl Harbor took place. The ship was then sent to the West Coast in March 1942. Upon arrival it was loaded with sixteen US Army Air Force B-25 Mitchell medium bombers, commanded by Lieutenant Colonel James H. 'Jimmy' Doolittle. After approaching the Japanese Home Islands, the medium bombers were launched in a one-way mission on 18 April 1942 in an attack known as the 'Doolittle Raid'.

The *Hornet* missed the Battle of the Coral Sea but did take part in the Battle of Midway, where her aircraft sank a Japanese cruiser and damaged a destroyer. During the follow-on Battle of the Santa Cruz Islands the ship's aircraft, along with those from the USS *Enterprise*, damaged a Japanese carrier and cruiser but did not sink either of them. In return, the Japanese carrier-based aircraft mounted a series of well-coordinated attacks on the USS *Hornet*. The ship was struck both by bombs and torpedoes, including two Japanese attackers who deliberately flew into the American carrier, a harbinger of the late-war kamikaze attacks.

After the *Hornet* lost all power due to the Japanese aerial attacks, it was ordered abandoned. Escorting US navy destroyers failed to sink the ship, despite repeated torpedo and gunfire attacks. It fell to approaching Japanese destroyers to finish off the job with their torpedoes and the USS *Hornet* finally slipped below the surface on 27 October 1942.

Experimental Support Carrier

While the Washington Naval Treaty restricted the number of fleet carriers that the US navy could have in service up to 1938, those few in service were considered extremely valuable assets that could not be employed on anything other than the most important assignments.

In 1939 the commanding officer of the USS *Ranger*, Captain John S. McCain, proposed in an unsolicited letter to the Secretary of the Navy that eight inexpensive but fast 'pocket-size' carriers be built. They were not intended to replace the larger fleet carriers. Rather, they would perform the more mundane secondary duties of escorting convoys, conducting anti-submarine operations and transporting aircraft.

At roughly the same time as this suggestion, the US navy's Bureau of Construction and Repair was considering plans to convert a number of passenger ships into small experimental supporting carriers. Both proposals were rejected by the US navy's senior leadership as being impractical.

However, in late 1940 President Franklin D. Roosevelt expressed interest in starting a programme to have suitable merchant ships converted into a fleet of small 6,000 to 8,000-ton supporting carriers. He also directed that these new carriers had to be constructed in a span of three months or less. In March 1941 the US navy senior leadership bowed to the president's wishes and acquired a merchant ship for conversion into a prototype supporting carrier.

As ordered by the president, the new supporting carrier was finished within the three-month authorized timeframe and commissioned in June 1941 as the USS *Long Island* (AVG-1). The three-letter suffix designation code 'AVG' stood for 'aircraft escort vessel'. The experimental ship was judged a success and would set the general pattern for the large number of small supporting carriers that followed.

The USS *Long Island* had a full load displacement of 13,499 tons and an overall length of 492 feet. It typically carried twenty aircraft that were moved between its unarmoured flight and hangar decks by a single centreline elevator. There was also a single hydraulically-operated flight deck catapult.

Entering service too late to see combat during the First World War, HMS *Argus* shown here prior to the Second World War was employed to test a number of components such as arresting gear. The carrier was decommissioned in the late 1920s and placed in storage. It was recommissioned by the Royal Navy shortly before the Second World War to act as a second-line training ship for pilots. *(Maritime Quest)*

The USS *Langley* (CV-1), the US navy's first carrier, was converted from a fleet collier named the USS *Jupiter* (AC-3) seen here in its original configuration. The ship had seen employment as a coal-hauling re-supply ship from 1913 until 1920. Note the many vertical booms, to which would be attached buckets which assisted in passing the coal stored within the ship's holds to a receiving dock or ship. *(NNAM)*

The masts seen here on a docked USS *Langley* were employed to string radio antenna wires and signal flags and were removable when the ship intended to launch and recover aircraft. In its original configuration, the ship had a stack mounted on either side of its rear hull as seen in this photograph. As the exhaust smoke from these stacks interfered with aircraft operations, they were replaced by two stacks on the port side of the ship that could be hinged downwards when needed. *(NNAM)*

The first unassisted launching of a plane from the USS *Langley* took place on 17 October 1922. The first recovery of an aircraft while the ship was under way occurred nine days later. Pictured is a Douglas DT-2 two-seat torpedo-bomber landing on the *Langley*. Approximately sixty-six DT-2s were built for the US navy, some of them serving on the carrier between 1922 and 1925. *(NNAM)*

(*Above*) A picture taken under the flight deck of the USS *Langley* shows the ship's main deck with a number of aircraft stored on it prior to either being brought up to the flight deck by the centreline elevator or lifted down into one of the carrier's holds by one of the overhead cranes seen at the top of the photograph. The *Langley* could carry as many as forty-two aircraft, with thirty being the average. (*RWP*)

(*Opposite above*) Visible in this photograph of the USS *Langley* is the carrier's single centreline elevator. The ship's flight deck was 534 feet long and 64 feet wide. Those involved in the early efforts at promoting the promise of naval aviation were not pleased with the ship's maximum speed of only 15.5 knots as this meant it would not be able to keep up with even the US navy's oldest and slowest battleships. However, they felt it was the best that could be had at the time. (*NNAM*)

(*Opposite below*) One of the features of the USS *Langley* seen here was the fact that the ship had turbo-electric drive. This was in contrast to the geared steam turbine engines found in most other US navy ships of the day. Because the ship had turbo-electric drive, it could steam astern as quickly as it sailed ahead. This meant that the carrier could, in theory, launch and recover planes at either end of the flight deck if one end was damaged. (*NNAM*)

(*Above*) A plane is shown preparing to land on the flight deck of the USS *Langley*. In this photograph we can see the later configuration of the ship's stacks, with both now being located together on the port side of the carrier. In this picture they are both hinged downwards so the exhaust gases will interfere less with the launching or recovery of aircraft. (*NNAM*)

(*Opposite page*) An unusual view of the USS *Langley* taken from an aircraft just launched from the ship. In its original configuration, the aircraft being recovered upon the ship's flight deck were guided to a safe landing by anchored longitudinal cables, raised and lowered by an electric motor. Eventually the ship's longitudinal cables were replaced with weighted transverse arresting cables. (*RWP*)

(*Left*) The USS *Langley*, having outlived its usefulness as an experimental carrier, was converted into a seaplane tender in 1936. In this new role, the ship became the USS *Langley* (AV-3). As seaplanes could not be launched or recovered from the ship's flight deck, it was cut back as is seen in the overhead photograph. Now visible is the ship's navigation bridge, formerly covered over by the flight deck. (*RWP*)

(*Above*) In the left-hand foreground of this picture, taken on the forward flight deck of the USS *Lexington* looking rearward, is an aircraft-handling crane. Behind the crane are two of the ship's four twin-8"/55 calibre gun armoured turrets located on armoured barbettes. Behind the superimposed (or super-firing) turret is the ship's navigation bridge surmounted by an armoured rangefinder. (*NA*)

(*Opposite above*) Pictured are two US navy admirals holding a large wooden model intended to show what a new class of six battle-cruisers, then under construction, would look like if they had been completed. Below that is another large wooden model showing the proposed appearance of two of the battle-cruisers when converted into carriers. The picture is dated 8 March 1922 and was taken before the Naval Affairs Committee of the US Congress. (*RWP*)

(*Opposite below*) The two cancelled battle-cruisers converted into carriers for the US navy were the USS *Lexington* (CV-2) and the USS *Saratoga* (CV-3), which formed the *Lexington* class. The unfinished hull of the *Lexington* was launched on 3 October 1925. It was then moved to its fitting-out pier as seen here, where it was completed. It was commissioned on 14 December 1927. (*RWP*)

(*Above*) From this aerial picture of the USS *Lexington* in 1929 can be seen the ship's island (superstructure) straddled by a tripod foremast that is topped off by the fire-control direction centres for the ship's large-calibre guns. Three of the twelve unarmoured pedestal mounts for the ship's 5"/25 calibre anti-aircraft guns can be seen just below the forward flight deck in an outward projecting sponson on the port side. (*NA*)

(*Opposite page*) This picture taken from the tripod foremast of the USS *Lexington* looking aft shows a windowed compartment affixed to the forward portion of the ship's large stack. This small compartment was referred to as the 'secondary conning station' and was a back-up navigation bridge if the one located in the ship's island was rendered inoperable. The open-topped space on the roof of the secondary conning station was the primary flight-control centre for the ship. (*NA*)

(*Above*) Looking forward from the stern of the flight deck of the USS *Lexington* can be seen the two twin-8"/55 calibre armoured gun turrets located aft of the ship's stack. Located above the superimposed turret is the aft fire-control direction centre for the ship's rear large-calibre guns. The aft fire-control direction centre was mounted on a stub mainmast attached to the ship's stack. (*NA*)

(*Opposite above*) Pictured on board the USS *Lexington* prior to the Second World War is one of the ship's two aft-mounted twin-8"/55 calibre gun armoured turrets engaging in a gunnery exercise. They were intended only for surface fire and did not have the elevation needed to fire at aerial targets. The four twin-8"/55 turrets were removed from the ship in early 1942. (*NA*)

(*Opposite below*) The USS *Lexington* in dry dock at Hunter's Point Naval Shipyard in San Francisco, California in April 1928. The ship's impressive flight deck was 880 feet long. As with the USS *Langley*, the ship's flight deck was originally fitted with electrically-powered longitudinal cables to prevent lightweight planes from veering off the flight deck upon landing. This system was removed in 1931 and replaced by hydraulically-controlled arresting cables arranged transversely across the flight deck. (*NA*)

(*Above*) Tugs are seen pushing the USS *Lexington* towards a pier in this 1929 picture taken in Panama. Visible in the picture at the bow of the ship are two of its three anchors and the hawse hole for the mooring lines. Life-nets are arranged around the outside of the flight deck to minimize the chances of sailors falling into the sea. Visible near the aft end of the hull, just below the flight deck, are four of the five cut-outs in the ship's hull for storage of the ship's boats. (*RWP*)

(*Opposite above*) Shown taking off from the stern of the USS *Lexington* is a Martin BM-1 dive-bomber, of which the US navy acquired sixteen units in the early 1930s with a follow-on order of sixteen slightly improved units designated the BM-2. Testing in the 1920s and 1930s convinced the US navy that dive-bombing was much more successful than horizontal bombing when attacking moving ships. Therefore the dive-bombers on US navy carriers were considered their most potent anti-ship weapon. (*NNAM*)

(*Opposite below*) Arranged in neat rows within the enclosed hangar deck of the USS *Lexington* are Curtiss F6C-3 Hawk single-seat fighters. The hangar deck on the ship was 450 feet long and 70 feet wide. The US navy bought thirty-five units of the Curtiss F6C-3 Hawk and they all served aboard the USS *Lexington* from 1927 till 1930. The plane had a maximum speed of 155 mph. (*NA*)

So large was the flight deck on the USS *Lexington*, seen here in this pre-Second World War picture, that its standard inventory of eighty aircraft could be stored on it and launched from it. This was partly driven by the small size of the ship's enclosed hangar deck. The sharply-tapered faired bow of the ship reflected its battle-cruiser heritage and led to the forward edge of the flight deck being extremely narrow. *(RWP)*

Because the USS *Lexington* had turbo-electric drive, as did the USS *Langley*, it could sail in reverse as fast as it could sail forward. To take advantage of that feature and to allow its onboard aircraft to both launch and recover on either end of the flight deck, it was decided to widen the forward portion of the ship's flight deck. This occurred between 1936 and 1937 and the result of that modification can be seen in this photograph. *(RWP)*

On the morning of 8 May 1942 during the Battle of the Coral Sea a Japanese force of sixty-nine aircraft located the USS *Lexington*. Despite the ship being protected by friendly fighter planes, it was mortally wounded by both enemy bombs and torpedoes. The picture shows the crew abandoning the listing ship upon its captain's orders on the afternoon of 8 May. Alongside the carrier is a US navy destroyer trying to rescue as many members of the ship's crew as possible. *(RWP)*

(*Above*) The sister ship of the USS *Lexington* was the USS *Saratoga*. It is seen here on the right of the picture in 1934 during an open house day for the public in New York Harbor. There were only some very minor external visual differences between the two *Lexington*-class carriers. Like its sister ship, the USS *Saratoga* was commissioned in 1927 and had a crew complement of approximately 2,120 officers and men. (*RWP*)

(*Opposite page*) Due to US navy concerns that pilots might be confused by the near-identical appearance of the two *Lexington*-class carriers when they were working together in reasonably close proximity, the abbreviated ships' names were eventually painted in large letters on the rear of their flight decks. An example of that pre-Second World War practice can be seen here on the USS *Saratoga* with the ship's name shortened to just 'SARA'. (*RWP*)

(*Below*) In the 1930s a large, solid black stripe was painted down the centre on either side of the massive stack of the USS *Saratoga*. This was done to assist pilots in distinguishing which *Lexington*-class carrier they were looking at prior to landing. (*RWP*)

Landing on the flight deck of the USS *Saratoga* is a Martin T4M-1 torpedo-bomber, which could also drop bombs when called upon. The three-man aircraft first entered US navy service in August 1928 on both *Lexington*-class carriers. A total of 102 units of the T4M-1 were acquired by the US navy and it remained in service until 1937. (*RWP*)

The USS *Saratoga* is shown in this pre-war picture. The carrier, like its sister ship the USS *Lexington*, had a permanently-assigned carrier air group (CAG) composed of four squadrons comprising a fighter, dive-bomber, torpedo-bomber and scouting squadron. The policy of assigning permanent air groups to US navy carriers ended in 1942. (*RWP*)

Shown in dry dock is the USS *Saratoga* with its very narrow forward flight deck, which was due to the sharply-tapered bow inherited from its battle-cruiser origins. To provide more room on the forward flight deck of the carrier, the US navy had plans to widen it as they had done in 1936 with the USS *Lexington*. However, as the clouds of war darkened in the late 1930s, the US navy was reluctant to commit the USS *Saratoga* to a shipyard for the period of time needed to rebuild the ship's bow. (NA)

(*Above*) The USS *Saratoga* finally got its widened bow in 1942, as seen here in this 1945 picture. Numerous other modifications were made to the ship in 1942, including the replacement of its four 8″/55 calibre twin-gun armoured turrets with four 5″/38 calibre twin-gun armoured mounts. The massive stack was shortened by 20 feet and the foremast that had supported the fire-control direction centre was discarded and replaced by a simple pole mast. (*NA*)

(*Opposite above*) On 21 February 1945 the USS *Saratoga* was attacked on two separate occasions by Japanese aircraft under the cover of inclement weather. The enemy planes performed a combination of conventional bomb and kamikaze attacks that inflicted a great deal of damage on the ship and caused significant loss of life but did not sink it. Pictured are the ship's damage-control parties dealing with a large fire on the forward flight deck. (*NA*)

(*Opposite below*) Following in the steps of the two very large *Lexington*-class carriers appeared the much smaller sole ship of the *Ranger* class, the USS *Ranger* (CV-4), seen here prior to the Second World War. Like the USS *Langley* (CV-1), the ship's stacks could be hinged downwards when aircraft were being launched and recovered from the flight deck. The USS *Ranger* had six stacks as shown in this picture, three on either side of the ship's rear hull. (*RWP*)

A stern view of the USS *Ranger* in 1935 shows the three stacks on the port side of the ship hinged downwards during flight operations. Rather than the turbo-electric drive of the USS *Langley* and the two *Lexington*-class carriers, the *Ranger* was fitted with geared steam turbine engines, powered by fuel oil-fired boilers. This was done because the ship's hull was too narrow to allow the larger space required by turbo-electric drive components. (*RWP*)

As a space-saving effort on the USS *Ranger*, experimental outriggers were placed along the borders of the ship's small flight deck to store additional aircraft as pictured here. The plane shown is a Boeing F4B-4 single-seat fighter and was one of seventy-four units built for the US navy in the early 1930s. It had a top speed of 189 mph and a range of 570 miles. It was armed with two .30 calibre machine guns and could carry a small bomb load. (*NA*)

The semi-open hangar deck on the USS *Ranger* is seen here, reflecting the US navy's policy of jamming as many aircraft as possible onto their carriers. The four pre-war squadrons assigned to the ship comprised a total of seventy-six planes, divided between thirty-six fighters, thirty-six dive-bombers that also did double duty as scout planes and four utility planes. There was no torpedo-bomber squadron assigned to the USS *Ranger* until late in its service career. (RWP)

Shown in this pre-Second World War photograph is the USS *Yorktown* (CV-5), one of the three carriers of the *Yorktown* class. As it looked very similar to its sister ship the USS *Enterprise* (CV-6), the USS *Yorktown* had a large letter 'Y' painted on both sides of its stack to assist pilots in recognizing their carrier. The islands on the *Yorktown*-class carriers were larger than those that preceded them. (NNAM)

With the introduction of the *Yorktown*-class carriers, the separation between the stack and the island disappeared, as seen in this pre-war photograph of the USS *Yorktown*. The stack has now been merged into the rear of the ship's island; the first US navy carrier with this design feature. The ship's island incorporated a large tripod foremast that would eventually be topped by a number of radar antennas. *(NNAM)*

A pre-war stern view of the USS *Yorktown*, that had geared steam turbine engines like the other ships in its class rather than turbo-electric drive engines. The US navy had lost interest in turbo-electric drive engines by this time due to their weight, size and cost. Like the turbo-electric drive engines on the USS *Langley* and the two *Lexington*-class carriers, the geared steam turbine engines in the *Yorktown*-class carriers received their power from fuel oil-fired boilers. *(RWP)*

Visible in this pre-war photograph of the USS *Enterprise* are the letters 'EN' painted on the aft end of the ship's flight deck. These were also painted on the forwardmost portion of the flight deck and was done to assist returning pilots in identifying their carrier rather than the near-identical USS *Yorktown* when operating in the same general area. *(RWP)*

The *Yorktown* class of carriers was originally provided with close-range anti-aircraft protection by an American-designed 1.1-inch anti-aircraft gun arranged in sets of four on an unarmoured power-operated pedestal mount. The guns on their pedestal mount were officially designated as the 1.1"/75 calibre Mark I. Service use showed that the guns lacked sufficient knockdown power to be effective and the powered pedestal mount proved unreliable and overly complex in construction. *(NA)*

(*Above*) A picture of the island on the USS *Enterprise* dated March 1944. Halfway up the most forward portion of the island are the circular portals of the ship's navigation bridge, with an open flying bridge on top of it. On the port side of the island is a small enclosed compartment jutting out which served as the primary flight-control centre (Pri-Fly) which had an open-topped enclosure on its roof. (*NA*)

(*Opposite page*) The *Yorktown*-class carriers were armed with a number of single unarmoured 5″/38 calibre dual-purpose pedestal gun mounts as seen here. The weapon fired a two-piece semi-fixed round power-rammed into the breech ring of the guns. The power-rammer was crucial in maintaining the weapon's high rate of fire. (*RWP*)

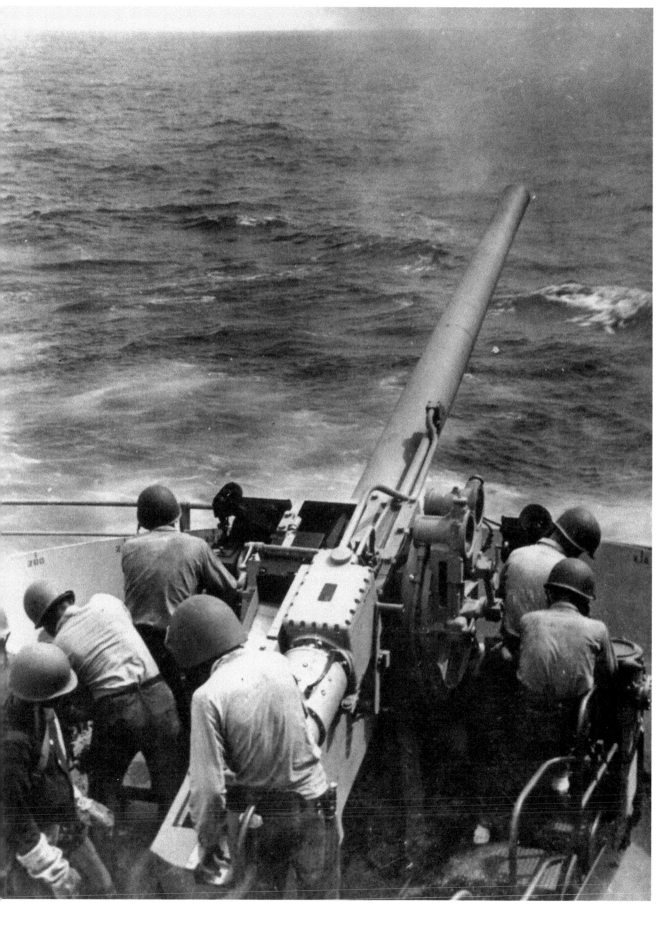

(*Above*) Taken some time in 1944 is this spectacular overhead view of the USS *Enterprise*. Like other ships in the *Yorktown* class, the *Enterprise* had a maximum speed of 33 knots. At the end of 1944, the ship was fitted out to operate night-capable air-defence fighter planes. During daylight hours, the carrier's flight deck was employed to recover planes damaged in combat that could not make it back to their own ships. (*RWP*)

(*Opposite above*) Taken from an aircraft that has just been launched is this view of the USS *Enterprise* in July 1944. Note how far the various forward anti-aircraft gun sponsons project out from either side of the ship's hull, just below the flight deck. By this time the carrier had had its 1.1"/75 calibre Mark I anti-aircraft gun batteries replaced by the much more reliable and powerful Swedish-designed Bofors 40mm anti-aircraft guns, licence-built in the United States. (*NA*)

(*Opposite below*) Pictured is the badly-damaged forward portion of the flight deck of the USS *Enterprise* on 14 May 1945, after being struck by a kamikaze just aft of the forward centreline elevator. A bomb from the kamikaze penetrated down to the ship's third deck and the resulting explosion blew the forward centreline elevator off the ship and caused a large fire on the hangar deck. The carrier was then sent back to the United States for repairs and did not see combat again. (*NA*)

U.S.S. HORNET (CV8) CLOSEUP VIEW, STBD SIDE, IN WAY
OF ISLAND, SHOWING ALTERED 36" SEARCHLIGHT PLATFORM
ACCESS LADDERS, DOCKING BRIDGE, LIFE RAFT STOWAGES
NEW 20MM BATTERY, FORD BOAT CRANE REMOVED, ETC.
NORFOLK NAVY YARD   PORTSMOUTH, VA.
PHOTO SERIAL 2789(42)   FEB. 28, 1942

(*Above*) Looking up from a dock is this picture dated 28 February 1942 of the island and the stack that merged into it on the USS *Hornet*. The ship's foretop, seen here from the rear and below, is saucer-shaped in comparison with the box-like appearance of the foretop of the other two *Yorktown*-class carriers. At the rear of the stack is a partial view of the large crane employed to lift aircraft from a dock or pier onto the ship's flight deck. (*RWP*)

(*Opposite above*) The USS *Hornet* (CV-8) was the last of the three *Yorktown*-class carriers and is seen here in this 27 October 1941 photograph, a week after her commissioning. Note that the ship's radar antennas have not yet been fitted to the tripod foremast. The carrier's island differs from the preceding two ships in its class. The forward sponson located on the starboard side of the ship, just below the flight deck, is missing its unarmoured 5"/38 calibre dual-purpose guns. (*RWP*)

(*Opposite below*) The USS *Hornet*'s foretop, the platform on the top of the tripod foremast, differed from those seen on the two earlier *Yorktown*-class carriers. The ship's first captain was Captain Marc A. Mitscher, one of the US navy's early naval aviation pioneers. Prior to taking command of the USS *Hornet* he had served on both the USS *Langley* (CV-1) and USS *Saratoga* (CV-3). (*RWP*)

(*Above*) Pictured taking off from the flight deck of the USS *Hornet* on 18 April 1942 is one of the sixteen US Army Air Force's North American B-25 Mitchell medium bombers that took part in the famous Doolittle Raid. The carrier was severely damaged by Japanese aerial attackers on 26 October 1942 during the Battle of the Santa Cruz Islands and sank later that same day. (*NA*)

(*Opposite above*) A pre-war picture of the USS *Wasp* (CV-7) during some type of naval review. Note that the much smaller stack of the carrier is partially enclosed by the ship's island, rather than being merged into the rear of the island as on the *Yorktown*-class carriers. Top speed of the ship was only 29.5 knots compared to the 33-knot maximum speed of the larger *Yorktown*-class carriers. (*RWP*)

(*Opposite below*) One of the novel new design features on the USS *Wasp* was a port-side deck-edge elevator. Rather than being a full-frame elevator platform, it was a large T-shaped platform with just enough room to carry a single aircraft but no personnel. It is seen here in operation pre-war with a two-seat Vought SB2U Vindicator bomber. (*NNAM*)

72-S-19   U.S.NAVY

(*Above*) Prior to the Japanese attack on Pearl Harbor, President Roosevelt had created a programme for converting civilian merchant ships into small support carriers. An experimental prototype of such a ship was the USS *Long Island* (AVG-1), seen here in autumn 1941 sailing off the East Coast of the United States. The letter suffix designation code 'AVG' stood for aircraft escort vessel but was later changed to 'CVE' for escort aircraft carrier. (*RWP*)

(*Opposite above*) A picture of the USS *Wasp* entering Hampton Roads, Virginia in May 1942, painted in a wartime scheme known as Measure 12 (Modified). This consisted of blues and greys and was in use from September 1941 until late 1942 or early 1943. It was also applied to the USS *Ranger* (CV-4) and the USS *Hornet* (CV-8). Its purpose was to provide a degree of concealment from both aerial and surface observation, as well as confusing optical rangefinders regarding the ships' range and heading. (*NNAM*)

(*Opposite below*) A dramatic image of the listing USS *Wasp* burning furiously after its fuel storage system had failed following three successful torpedo strikes on the ship by a Japanese submarine on 15 September 1942. Due to treaty restrictions regarding authorized displacement tonnage, the ship went into service with no side hull belt armour, although design provisions were made to install such belt armour if war arose. (*RWP*)

Chapter Two

Wartime Aircraft Carriers

As the first of the planned *Essex*-class carriers was not projected to enter service until early 1944 the US navy, at the strong urging of President Franklin D. Roosevelt in October 1941, came up with a stopgap plan to convert nine unfinished *Cleveland*-class light cruisers into light carriers designated 'CVL' with the letter 'L' standing for light. These went on to form the *Independence* class of carriers.

The first *Independence*-class carrier, commissioned in January 1943, was the USS *Independence* (CVL-22). The remaining eight (CVL-23 through CVL-30) entered US navy service that same year with the last, the USS *San Jacinto* (CVL-30) commissioned in December. The *Independence*-class vessels were never referred to as fleet carriers but always as light carriers.

The *Independence* class had a full load displacement of 15,100 tons with an overall length of 622 feet 6 inches. They typically carried thirty aircraft that were moved between the flight deck and the hangar deck by two centreline elevators. There was an armoured deck located below the ship's unarmoured hangar deck. A single hydraulically-operated flight deck catapult was originally fitted to the *Independence*-class carriers.

The *Independence*-class ships were not originally intended to have islands, as their flight deck space was at a premium. However, in a last-minute decision the US navy concluded that an island was needed. Therefore a small island was built on the side of the flight deck of the *Independence*-class carriers and not on the flight deck as on previous US navy carriers.

Of the nine *Independence*-class carriers commissioned, only the USS *Princeton* (CVL-23) was lost to enemy action. On 24 October 1944 during the Battle of Leyte Gulf an enemy bomb penetrated its flight and hangar decks and exploded on the ship's armoured deck. The resulting aviation fuel fire spread and detonated the ship's onboard torpedo magazine. After being abandoned by its crew, the badly-damaged carrier was sunk by an escorting US navy cruiser and destroyer.

Although they were a far from perfect solution, the *Independence*-class carriers performed an important role in holding the line against the Japanese navy in 1943 and early 1944. Due to the light cruiser machinery they had inherited, the *Independence*-class vessels could sail alongside the faster ships of the US navy during the Second

World War, such as the *Essex*-class fleet carriers, except when they were sailing at their maximum speed.

Essex-Class Carriers

The second carrier ordered under the Congressional-approved Naval Expansion Act of 1938 after the USS *Hornet* was the USS *Essex* (CV-9). Unlike the *Hornet* that was built as a near-copy of the first two *Yorktown*-class carriers to speed up its construction and entry into fleet service, the USS *Essex* was something new and was the first US navy carrier not restricted in its displacement tonnage by the Washington Naval Treaty. The ship was laid down in April 1941 and commissioned in December 1942. It did not reach the Pacific until May 1943 and saw its first combat action in August 1943.

Clearly owing its roots to the design of the *Yorktown*-class carriers, the USS *Essex* reflected the US navy's desire for a better protected fleet carrier with an increased operational range. It also had to have a much longer and wider flight and hangar deck, in order to operate an increased number of aircraft that would be both larger and heavier than those currently in service. To meet these requirements, the USS *Essex* was both bigger and heavier than the preceding *Yorktown*-class carriers, with a full load displacement of 33,000 tons.

The *Essex* had an overall length of 872 feet and typically carried 100 aircraft. There was only one hydraulically-operated flight deck catapult installed on the ship sometime between April and May 1943. It did not see much use until the later stages of the Second World War when the next generation of larger and heavier carrier prop-driven aircraft began making their appearance. However, the flight deck catapult did prove useful in situations where wind conditions were unfavourable to the launching of carrier aircraft employing the typical rolling take-off into the wind. A second hydraulically-operated flight deck catapult was added to the USS *Essex* following the Second World War.

The aircraft on the USS *Essex* were moved between the flight deck and the hangar deck by three elevators, two being centerline and the third a deck edge elevator located on the port-side (left) amidships. It was a larger and more capable version than that installed on the USS *Wasp*.

Captain Donald B. Duncan, USS *Essex*'s first commanding officer, was very pleased with his ship's deck-edge elevator. In a positive report to his superiors he wrote:

Since there is no large hole in [the] flight deck when the elevator is on the 'down' position, it is easier to continue normal operations on deck, irrespective of the position of the elevator. The elevator increases the effective space when it is in the 'up' position by providing additional parking room outside the normal contours of the flight deck, and increases the effective area on the hangar deck by the absence of elevator pits.

Essex-Class Build-Up

The German military invasion of Poland on 1 September 1939 was the official start of the Second World War but failed to prompt the US government to fund the building of additional fleet carriers for the US navy. This reflected the powerful isolationist feeling that still coursed through American domestic politics. It took the German military invasion of France and the Low Countries in May 1940 to push the US Congress into action. On 10 July 1940 President Franklin D. Roosevelt signed the Two-Ocean Navy Act which provided the funding for the construction of three additional *Essex*-class carriers.

The three carriers authorized were the USS *Yorktown* (CV-10), USS *Intrepid* (CV-11) and USS *Hornet* (CV-12), two of them being named in honour of their sunken predecessors. All three carriers were commissioned in 1943; however, only the USS *Yorktown* made it to the Pacific in time to see combat that year. The other two would not enter action until 1944: the USS *Intrepid* in January and the USS *Hornet* in March.

US Congress then authorized the building of another seven *Essex*-class carriers in July 1940. These comprised the USS *Franklin* (CV-13), USS *Ticonderoga* (CV-14), USS *Randolph* (CV-15), USS *Lexington* (CV-16), USS *Bunker Hill* (CV-17), USS *Wasp* (CV-18) and USS *Hancock* (CV-19). All were commissioned between 1943 and 1944. As before, two of them bore the names of earlier US navy carriers lost in battle. The USS *Lexington* and USS *Bunker Hill* would see combat in 1943, with the remainder not doing so until 1944 and 1945.

Following the Japanese attack on Pearl Harbor on 7 December 1941, Congress funded the building of two more *Essex*-class carriers, the USS *Bennington* (CV-20) and the USS *Boxer* (CV-21), the first being commissioned in 1944 and the second in 1945. The USS *Bennington* took part in the invasion and conquest of Iwo Jima between February and March 1945. In April 1945 the ship's aircraft assisted in sinking the Japanese navy battleship IJN *Yamato*. The USS *Boxer* did not see action during the Second World War.

In August 1942 Congress authorized the construction of ten more *Essex*-class carriers, which included CV-31 through CV-40 (hull numbers 22 to 30 had been reserved by the US navy for another class of carriers). Congress released funding for building the last three *Essex*-class carriers in June 1943. These were CV-45 through CV-47, hull numbers 41 through 44 having been reserved for another class of carriers.

Of the twenty-six *Essex*-class carriers authorized by Congress between 1938 and 1943, two were cancelled before completion: the *Reprisal* (CV-35) and the *Iwo Jima* (CV-46). Of the remaining twenty-four commissioned, only fourteen reached the Pacific in time to see combat action against the Japanese.

None of the fourteen *Essex*-class carriers that went into combat during the Second World War was sunk. A few did suffer heavy damage due to enemy action, such as the USS *Franklin* that was struck by two bombs on 19 March 1945. The semi-armour-piercing bombs punched through the ship's flight deck and exploded on the armoured hangar deck. Personnel losses on the ship totalled 724 killed and 265 wounded. The USS *Ticonderoga* and USS *Bunker Hill* both suffered heavy damage and large loss of life due to kamikaze strikes in 1945.

Within the *Essex* class of carriers there was a single subtype, labelled as the 'long-hull' design by many, featuring a sharper angle clipper bow. This meant that the overall length of these ships was 888 feet, 16 feet longer than those *Essex*-class carriers without the clipper bows. Of the twenty-four *Essex*-class carriers eventually commissioned, eleven were the long-hull subtype, four of which saw service in the Second World War. The remaining long-hull versions were concentrated in the last two batches authorized.

Lessons learned from combat in the Pacific and design improvements by the builders resulted in a number of modifications to the *Essex* class during the Second World War. These primarily revolved around the number of catapults, the arrangement of the island and the navigation bridge, anti-aircraft defences and the electronic devices (radar) and antennas mounted on the ships, all of which pushed up their full load displacement.

Follow-on Support Carrier

Falling into a separate one-ship class with the US navy was the carrier USS *Charger* (AVG-30). Based on a passenger/cargo ship, the vessel, together with three of its sister ships, was originally intended to be transferred to the Royal Navy under the Lend-Lease programme. However, at the last moment the transfer of this one converted ship out of the four was rescinded and it spent its entire time in service with the US navy.

The USS *Charger* was commissioned in US navy service in March 1942. It had a full load displacement of 15,900 tons, an overall length of 492 feet and carried fifteen aircraft. Planes were moved between the unarmoured flight and hangar decks by two centreline elevators. The ship never saw action as it was retained as a training ship on the East Coast of the United States throughout the Second World War.

In August 1942 the *Charger* was re-designated as an auxiliary aircraft carrier (ACV). In July 1943 the ship was once again re-designated, this time as an escort aircraft carrier (CVE). The same letter suffix designation code change was also applied to all civilian ships converted to carriers, including the USS *Long Island* that eventually became CVE-1.

The letter suffix designation code CVE was also later applied to small purpose-built carriers that would perform the same roles as the civilian ships converted into support carriers. For the sake of convenience all of the escort carriers mentioned hereafter will bear the CVE letter suffix code.

Reflecting the often morbid sense of humour of those going into harm's way, the sailors assigned to serve in the CVEs believed the letter suffix designation code really stood for 'Combustible, Vulnerable and Expendable'. Many in the US navy would refer to the CVEs as 'Jeep carriers', while the American press nicknamed them 'baby flat tops'.

Sangamon-Class Carriers

As there was a shortage of merchant ships, following the commissioning of the experimental USS *Long Island* (AVG-1) in June 1941 the US navy decided to convert four *Cimarron*-class fleet oilers into escort carriers. All four were commissioned between August and September 1942 as the *Sangamon* class. These comprised the USS *Sangamon* (CVE-26), USS *Suwannee* (CVE-27), USS *Chenango* (CVE-28) and USS *Santee* (CVE-29).

The *Sangamon* class had a full load displacement of 24,275 tons and an overall length of 553 feet. Their thirty aircraft were moved between the unarmoured flight and hangar decks by two centreline elevators. A single hydraulically-operated flight deck catapult was fitted to these carriers.

Bogue-Class Carriers

At the same time that the four *Sangamon*-class escort carriers were being constructed, American shipyards had already begun work on converting forty-five merchant ships into a new class of escort carrier (CVE). Commissioned between September 1942 and April 1943, these ships were referred to as the *Bogue* class (CVE-9 through CVE-25 and CVE-31 through CVE-54).

Of the forty-five *Bogue*-class escort carriers built, thirty-four were transferred to the Royal Navy. Of the eleven retained by the US navy only one, the USS *Block Island* (CVE-21), was lost to enemy action during the Second World War, being sunk by a German submarine.

The *Bogue*-class escort carriers had an overall length of 495 feet 8 inches and a full load displacement of 15,700 tons. They typically carried twenty aircraft moved between the unarmoured flight and hangar decks by two centreline elevators. There was a single hydraulically-operated flight deck catapult. In Royal Navy service the *Bogue*-class vessels featured a number of additional safety features insisted upon by the Royal Navy, which raised the ships' full load displacement.

Casablanca-Class Carriers

The *Bogue* class was followed by the construction of fifty *Casablanca*-class escort carriers (CVE-55 through CVE-104), making them the most numerous carriers built in history by any country. Unlike the escort carriers that went before them based on the conversion of existing ships, the *Casablanca*-class escort carriers were mass-produced from the keel up by American shipbuilder Henry J. Kaiser.

All of the *Casablanca*-class escort carriers were commissioned between July 1942 and July 1944 and served solely with the US navy during the Second World War. The *Casablanca*-class carriers were also referred to as the Kaiser-class CVEs. A popular, if unkind, nickname often used by those who served on these ships was 'Kaiser's coffins'.

The *Casablanca*-class escort carriers had an overall length of 512 feet 3 inches and a full load displacement of 10,400 tons. They typically carried thirty aircraft. Planes were moved between the flight and unarmoured hangar decks by two centreline elevators. The flight deck had two hydraulically-operated catapults.

Two of the *Casablanca* class, the USS *St. Lo* (CVE-63) and the USS *Gambier Bay* (CVE-73), were lost to enemy action during the Battle of Samar on 25 October 1944. This was one of four major naval engagements that took place during the Battle of Leyte Gulf which ran from 23 to 26 October 1944. The *St. Lo* was sunk by a kamikaze attack and the *Gambier Bay* by naval surface fire. Three others were also lost to enemy action during the Second World War.

Commencement Bay-Class Carriers

The *Casablanca*-class escort carriers were followed into production by the *Commencement Bay* class. Unlike their predecessors, this last class of escort carriers was constructed by converting tanker hulls. The US navy originally ordered thirty-five ships of the class but only nineteen were actually built. Of those nineteen, only thirteen (CVE-105 through CVE-117) were completed before the conclusion of the Second World War, with the USS *Commencement Bay* (CVE-105) and USS *Long Island* (CVE-106) being commissioned in late 1944 and the remaining ships in 1945. A few saw some service near the closing stages of the war in the Pacific.

The *Commencement Bay*-class escort carriers had a full load displacement of 24,750 tons, with an overall length of 557 feet 6 inches. They typically carried fifty aircraft that were moved between the unarmoured flight and hangar decks by two centreline elevators. The flight deck was fitted with two hydraulically-operated catapults.

As a wartime stopgap measure suggested by President Roosevelt, the US navy had nine of its *Cleveland*-class light cruisers converted into *Independence*-class carriers. These ships were intended to fill a gap in the carrier ranks until the *Essex*-class carriers were in service. As carriers, the *Independence* class was designated by the letter suffix designation code 'CVL', with the letter 'L' standing for 'light'. The first in the class was the USS *Independence* (CVL-22), seen here. (*NNAM*)

The second ship in the *Independence* class of carriers was the USS *Princeton* (CVL-23), shown here and commissioned on 25 February 1943. It first saw combat in September 1943. It and the USS *Independence* were not fitted with the hull belt armour that all the *Cleveland* light cruisers were intended to have, as there was a shortage of armoured steel at the time they were being constructed. (*RWP*)

Pictured is the launching of the USS *Belleau Wood* (CVL-24) on 6 December 1942. All nine of the *Independence*-class carriers were built at the New York Shipbuilding Corporation located in Camden, New Jersey. They had a top speed of 31 knots, which was 2 knots slower than the *Essex*-class carriers that were to follow but did not really hinder them from working alongside the *Essex* class. (*RWP*)

(*Above*) A picture taken from the island of the USS *Belleau Wood* in late 1943, showing the aft flight deck of the ship during a very dramatic time. Parked on the port side of the flight deck are a number of Grumman F6F Hellcat fighters and on the starboard side are more than half a dozen Grumman-designed TBF Avenger torpedo-bombers. (*NNAM*)

(*Opposite page*) The island of the USS *Cabot* (CVL-28), commissioned in July 1943, is seen here. The rectangular antenna at the forwardmost portion of the ship's foremast is for the SK-2 back-up air-search radar system. The main SK air-search radar antenna was mounted on a stub main mast forward of the second pair of the carrier's four stacks. (*RWP*)

Painted on the side of the island of the USS *Langley* (CVL-27) is a scoreboard of the ship's accomplishments. On the left are enemy planes destroyed in aerial combat, next are bombing missions against land targets, then the number of enemy military and civilian ships sunk and finally, the number of enemy aircraft destroyed on the ground. (*RWP*)

Located on the port side of the aft flight deck of the USS *Langley*, and on every other US navy carrier during the Second World War, was a platform as seen here upon which stood the landing signal officer (LSO). It was his job to direct planes safely back to their ships. Table tennis-size paddles were employed to give directions and corrections to incoming pilots on their altitude, speed and the position of the aircraft with reference to the centreline of the carrier. (*NNAM*)

In the foreground of the picture is the USS *Langley*, which saw its first combat action in January 1944. Behind it is the USS *Ticonderoga* (CV-14), an *Essex*-class carrier. Very evident in the photograph is the much broader beam and larger island on the *Essex*-class carrier compared to that on the *Independence* class. *(NA)*

The *Independence*-class carriers were armed with nine 40mm gun twin mounts arranged in sponsons around the perimeter of the ship's hull, located just below flight-deck level. Two of the nine mounts on the USS *Independence* are shown here in a picture dated 30 April 1943. *(RWP)*

(*Above*) On 30 October 1944 a kamikaze struck the aft end of the flight deck of the USS *Belleau Wood* and caused a serious fire among the aircraft stored there, as seen in this picture. The flight-deck crewmen are pictured trying to move aircraft away from the fire and a damage-control team already has a fire hose in play. (*RWP*)

(*Opposite above*) The USS *Langley* is seen here in this wartime picture being overflown by a US navy K-Class blimp (airship), which was employed on anti-submarine patrols. The American firm Goodyear built 150 of these between 1942 and 1945. The flight decks on the *Independence*-class carriers were 552 feet long and 73 feet wide, while the hangar decks were 285 feet long and 55 feet wide. (*RWP*)

(*Opposite below*) Pictured is the USS *Essex* (CV-9) during its sea trials prior to commissioning. It was launched in July 1942. Note the port-side deck-edge elevator is in its upward stored position. This was the first carrier in the twenty-four-ship *Essex* class and when commissioned on 31 December 1942, it was the largest displacement US navy carrier built from the keel up. (*NNAM*)

(*Above*) Pictured at Newport News Shipbuilding, Virginia is the USS *Yorktown* (CV-10) prior to launch in January 1943 and commissioning in April 1943. The carrier would be the first in its class to see action against the Japanese in August 1943 during the Marcus Island Raid. It would also take part in the attack on Truk in February 1944 with eight other carriers, which claimed 270 Japanese aircraft for the loss of only twenty-one US navy carrier planes. (*RWP*)

(*Opposite above*) The air group assigned to the USS *Essex* is seen on the ship's flight deck during the Second World War. The aircraft at the rear of the flight deck are Douglas SBD Dauntless dive-bombers. The metal outriggers seen projecting from the starboard side of the carrier's hull are radio masts, which were raised when flight operations were not being conducted. (*Maritime Quest*)

(*Opposite below*) Inside the hangar deck of the USS *Essex* in June 1944 are stored examples of both the Curtiss SB2C Helldivers dive-bomber as well as the Grumman F6F Hellcat fighter. In 1942 the US navy began designating carrier groups by numbers rather than by the ships they had been assigned to. In the summer of 1944 the US navy began to identify air groups based on the type of carrier they were assigned to. (*RWP*)

(*Above*) This picture taken in May 1943 on the USS *Essex* shows members of the ship's crew engaging in target practice with their Swiss-designed 20mm Oerlikon anti-aircraft guns. In this configuration, the weapon and mount were referred to by the US navy as the 20mm single mount Mark 4. It proved to be an extremely reliable weapon and required no external power source. (*RWP*)

(*Opposite above*) The crew of a 20mm anti-aircraft gun takes a break at their post on board a US navy carrier during the Second World War. The *Essex*-class carriers were originally designed to mount forty-six of these short-range weapons. This went up to fifty-eight on some of them in the summer of 1943. The majority of the 20mm anti-aircraft guns fitted on the *Essex*-class carriers were mounted on catwalks located around and just below the flight deck. (*RWP*)

(*Opposite below*) To increase the accuracy of the 20mm anti-aircraft gun as found on the wartime *Essex*-class carriers, they were eventually fitted with the Mk. 14 gyro lead computing sight as seen here mounted on the top of the weapon's rear breech, just in front of the gunner. Prior to the introduction of the Mk. 14, the weapon was aimed by observing the trajectory of the projectiles in flight through a metal ring sight. (*RWP*)

(*Above*) As the Japanese began using kamikaze attacks in the later stages of the Second World War, the small projectile fired by the 20mm single mount Mk. 4 and its lack of knockdown power became an issue. To maintain the combat effectiveness of the 20mm anti-aircraft gun, the US navy tried multiple gun mounts with a twin-gun mount shown here that began appearing on carriers in early 1945. (*NA*)

(*Opposite page*) The medium-range anti-aircraft gun on the *Essex*-class carriers during the Second World War was the Swedish-designed 40mm Bofors gun, fitted in quadruple mounts. An example is seen here on the USS *Hornet* (CV-12) in February 1945. The *Essex*-class carriers were originally intended to be fitted with eight of the 40mm quadruple mounts but by the war's end there were up to eighteen of them. (*NA*)

A sailor is shown in an ammunition magazine of a US navy ship. He is passing up a four-round clip of 40mm ammunition to another sailor. The 40mm quadruple anti-aircraft mounts on the *Essex*-class carriers could fire a variety of rounds including high-explosive and armour-piercing. Each 40mm gun on the quadruple or twin anti-aircraft mounts was capable of firing up to 160 rounds per minute. *(NA)*

Pictured is a 40mm quadruple anti-aircraft mount and crew on the wartime *Essex*-class carrier the USS *Hancock* (CV-19). US navy shipboard anti-aircraft gunfire took fewer rounds to destroy enemy aircraft earlier in the war than later, according to a post-war US navy study. This was attributed to a number of reasons, including an increase in the number of enemy night attacks during which fire control was less accurate and the increase in speed and manoeuvrability of late-war enemy planes. *(NA)*

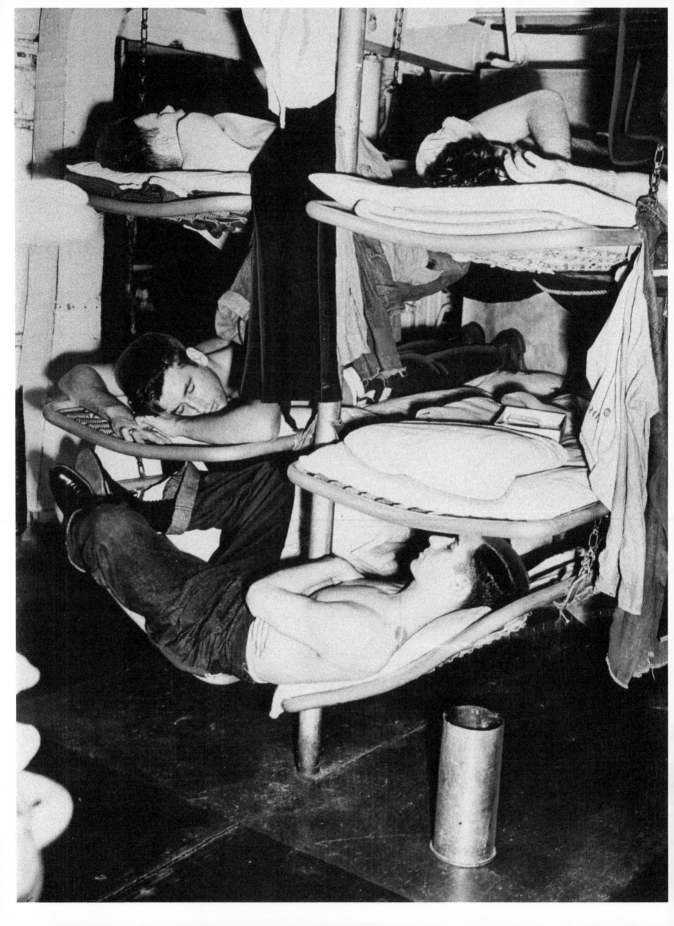

(*Opposite page*) The addition of ever-increasing numbers of labour-intensive anti-aircraft guns on *Essex*-class carriers late in the war resulted in serious overcrowding on the ships. The designers had never envisioned the number of personnel eventually assigned to the carriers. This picture shows the very uncomfortable sleeping arrangements on a wartime US navy ship. (*NA*)

(*Right*) Long-range anti-aircraft protection was provided to the wartime *Essex*-class carriers by twelve 5"/38 calibre dual-purpose guns. Eight of the guns were divided between four twin armoured gun mounts, with an example seen in this illustration from a US navy manual. The typical rate of fire for the four twin armoured gun mounts was fifteen rounds per minute per twin mount.

(*Below*) Shown at Newport News Shipyard in June 1943 is this starboard quarter view of the USS *Yorktown* (CV-10). Visible just behind the ship's island are two of the four 5"/38 calibre dual-purpose twin armoured gun mounts, the other two being located forward of the island. Due to the weight of the rounds fired by the guns, hydraulic piston rods drove a shell guard (also called a spade or shoe) which rammed the cartridge cases and the projectiles into the breech ring of the guns. (*RWP*)

GUN PORT SHIELD

SHIEL[

POWER-DRIVE CONTROLS

READY SERVICE POWDER

HANDLING ROOM

POWDER HOIST

LOWER AMMUNITION HOIST

PROJECTILE HOIST

CENTRAL COLUMN

LOWER AMMUNITION HOIST

Of the twelve 5"/38 calibre dual-purpose guns on wartime *Essex*-class carriers, four were in open unprotected pedestal mounts divided between two sponsons under the flight deck on the port side of the hull. This arrangement is seen here on the USS *Antietam* (CV-36) test-firing its pedestal-mounted 5"/38 calibre guns in March 1945. The ship arrived too late to see combat in the Second World War. *(RWP)*

The gunfire of the *Essex*-class carrier's 5"/38 calibre guns was normally aimed by two armoured fire-control directors mounted on barbettes, an example of which is seen here from a US navy manual. They acquired targets either using optical devices or radar guidance, as is evident from the radar antenna on top of the director shown. One of the two directors was mounted on top of the carrier's island and the other aft of the ship's stack.

RADAR ANTENNA

OBSERVATION HATCH (closed)

SLEWING SIGHT

TELESCOPE PORTS

RANGEFINDER

RANGEFINDER

BARBETTE

The data collected by the various optical and electronic sensors mounted on the wartime *Essex*-class carriers was fed into the Combat Information Center (CIC), an example of which is seen here on the USS *Wasp* (CV-18) during the Second World War. It was here that all the information was manually processed and presented to the ship's command staff to determine a course of action, such as when to engage incoming enemy aircraft. *(NA)*

The twelve large-calibre 5"/38 guns on the *Essex*-class carriers were not fired from the ship's Combat Information Center. Rather, once the decision was made by the ship's command staff to engage the enemy, that information was passed to the carrier's central fire-control room, also known as the 'gun plot'. An example of a gun plot is seen here in this October 1943 picture taken on board the USS *Yorktown* (CV-10). *(RWP)*

(*Above*) Pictured on board a wartime *Essex*-class carrier is the ship's radio room, an important command and control tool. There are, however, a couple of disadvantages in sending radio messages. First, they can be intercepted by the enemy, although this can be overcome to a certain extent by encrypting outgoing messages. Second, the use of long-range radios enables the enemy to use direction-finding devices to determine the location of the sending station. (*RWP*)

(*Opposite above*) The USS *Ticonderoga* (CV-14) was commissioned on 8 May 1944, was the tenth ship in the *Essex* class to be completed and the second long-hull version to enter into service. It is seen here in a dazzle camouflage paint scheme aimed at confusing submarine optical rangefinders. Two of the ship's elevators can be seen in this picture: the open rear flight-deck elevator and the port-side deck-edge elevator, which is folded upwards. (*NNAM*)

(*Opposite below*) A Grumman TBF Avenger torpedo-bomber is being loaded onto one of the two main flight-deck elevators of the wartime *Essex*-class carrier USS *Lexington* (CV-16). Each main flight-deck elevator was capable of moving aircraft up to 28,000lb. The smaller port-side deck-edge elevators could only handle 18,000lb. (*RWP*)

(*Above*) On the aft section of the flight deck of the wartime USS *Yorktown* (CV-10) is an assemblage of aircraft. Coming up on the elevator is a Grumman F6F Hellcat fighter, as is the aircraft in the foreground. In the right background is a Grumman TBF Avenger torpedo-bomber. At the rear of the flight deck are Curtiss SBC Helldiver dive-bombers, the replacements for the Douglas SBD Dauntless dive-bombers. (*NNAM*)

(*Opposite above*) There was a standard wheeled towing tug employed on wartime *Essex*-class carriers to move aircraft around, referred to at the time as a 'flight deck taxi'. However, in a pinch, stripped-down Jeeps were pressed into the role as seen in this 1945 photograph taken on the flight deck of the USS *Hornet* (CV-12), commissioned on 29 November 1943. (*RWP*)

(*Opposite below*) On the flight deck of an *Essex*-class carrier during the Second World War, ordnance men are shown wheeling out bombs on small dollies to waiting aircraft. These bombs were typically loaded onto carrier dive-bombers. Dive-bombing was adopted by the US navy in 1928 because it was more accurate than the existing level or horizontal bombing. (*NA*)

(*Above*) Ordnance men on an *Essex*-class carrier are shown loading a bomb onto a Douglas SBD Dauntless dive-bomber. The first two letters in the prefix designation code stand for scout-bomber, with the letter 'D' identifying the plane as a Douglas product. Note the bomb cradle that would swing out from the bottom of the aircraft's fuselage as it was in a dive and ready to drop its ordnance. (*NNAM*)

(*Opposite above*) A Grumman F6F Hellcat fighter pilot is shown revving up his engine on the flight deck of the USS *Yorktown* (CV-10) in late 1943. He is awaiting the signal from the flight-deck dispatcher seen holding a chequered flag. Once the flag was dropped, it signalled to the pilot to launch his aircraft. The Hellcat accounted for 4,987 Japanese aircraft during the Second World War. (*NA*)

(*Opposite below*) To assist in the launching of aircraft from the flight decks of the *Essex*-class carriers, some of the early production ships had been fitted with two hydraulically-operated catapults: one located on the flight deck and the other in the hangar deck. The hangar-deck catapult was mounted athwartships (in a direction at right angles to the centreline of the ship) and is shown here aiding in the launch of a Grumman F6F Hellcat fighter. (*NNAM*)

(*Above*) As the Japanese Empire continued to contract under American military pressure in 1944 and 1945, the Japanese became ever more desperate. One of the prime targets of their wrath was the numerous *Essex*-class carriers that were approaching ever closer to their homeland. It was at these ships that they launched their kamikazes, beginning in 1944. Pictured is the *Essex*-class carrier USS *Bunker Hill* (CV-17) after being struck in quick succession by two kamikazes on 11 May 1945. (*NA*)

(*Opposite above*) Once an attack was completed, the most harrowing moment for all carrier pilots was in safely landing their aircraft back aboard their ship. To assist pilots in returning to the correct vessel when more than one *Essex*-class carrier was operating in the same general area, the US navy had the ship's number painted on the forward and aft end of their flight decks, beginning in late 1943. Pictured is a Curtiss SBC Helldiver dive-bomber preparing for recovery on the USS *Yorktown* seen in the distance. (*NA*)

(*Opposite below*) Landing on a carrier's flight deck – a constantly moving object as it pitches and dips through the sea – is not for the faint-hearted, especially when a plane has been damaged in combat or the pilot has been wounded in action. Ever-changing environmental conditions can also make the task even more dangerous. Pictured is an example of what can happen when a recovery goes bad: an upside-down Grumman F6F-6 Hellcat lies on the flight deck of an *Essex*-class carrier. (*NNAM*)

A picture of the USS *Bunker Hill* with fires raging after being hit by two kamikazes on 11 May 1945, with a US navy *Cleveland*-class light cruiser standing by to render assistance. The ship survived the enemy attacks but with the loss of 346 men killed and another 264 wounded. US navy post-war studies identified 999 Japanese planes as kamikazes during the last two years of the Second World War. (NA)

Sailors look at the large dent made in the flight deck of their *Essex*-class carrier, the USS *Intrepid* (CV-11), by a kamikaze strike on 25 November 1944. The carrier was actually struck by two kamikazes that day, which caused enough damage to render the ship unfit for service but did not sink it. Sent back to the United States for repairs, it returned to the fighting in the Pacific in March 1945. (NA)

A look at the damage to a 20mm anti-aircraft gun battery on the port side of the USS *Essex* (CV-9) inflicted by a single kamikaze strike on 25 November 1944. Due to the location of the damage, flight operations on the ship were only interrupted for a very short time. Kamikaze pilots were instructed to crash their aircraft into the islands of US navy carriers to take out the ship's command and control functions or the carrier's elevators. *(RWP)*

(*Above*) On 21 January 1945 the *Essex*-class carrier USS *Ticonderoga* (CV-14) was struck by two kamikazes that caused extensive damage to the ship, killed 143 men and wounded another 202. The ship is seen here shortly after being hit by the kamikazes. The carrier is not listing due to the damage caused by the enemy: rather, ballast water has been added to the port side of the ship's hull to create the list. This was done so that all the water employed to fight the hangar-deck fires would drain out of the carrier and help wash the fire overboard. (*RWP*)

(*Opposite above*) The *Essex*-class carrier to suffer the most extensive damage during the Second World War was the USS *Franklin* (CV-13), seen here from the superstructure of another US navy ship which is attempting to render assistance. On 19 March 1945 two large Japanese aerial-delivered bombs penetrated into the ship's hangar deck and detonated while planes were being armed and fuelled. The resulting explosions and fires killed 807 men and wounded another 487. (*NA*)

(*Opposite below*) A picture taken from the island of the USS *Franklin* as it sails into New York Harbor in April 1945 shows the torn-up forward flight deck. There were plans to repair and modernize the carrier but none came to fruition. The ship was eventually decommissioned in 1947 and scrapped in 1966. (*NA*)

(*Above*) A non-combat threat to *Essex*-class carriers during the Second World War was the ravages of the weather. Pictured is the USS *Hornet*'s (CV-12) forward flight deck that collapsed during a typhoon in June 1945. It was the only serious damage suffered by the carrier during the Second World War. The vessel is currently preserved as a museum ship in Alameda, California. (*RWP*)

(*Opposite page*) Besides death by enemy action, there were many other ways to lose one's life on a wartime *Essex*-class carrier. Pictured is a burial at sea conducted on 22 January 1945 from the USS *Hancock* (CV-19). The day before, two 500lb bombs on a returning Grumman TBF Avenger torpedo-bomber exploded as it landed on the ship's flight deck, killing fifty members of the crew and wounding another seventy-five. (*RWP*)

(*Below*) The USS *Yorktown* (CV-10), an *Essex*-class carrier, is shown steaming off the Japanese island of Kyushu on 18 March 1945 with other US navy ships. On this date sixteen carriers of Task Force 58 under the command of Vice Admiral Marc A. Mitscher began launching air strikes to neutralize Japanese air power prior to the American invasion of Okinawa on 1 April 1945. In five days of operation, US naval aviators destroyed 482 enemy aircraft. (*NNAM*)

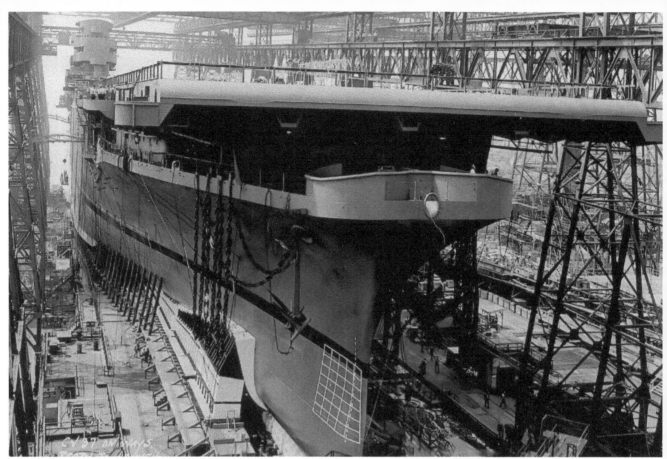

Even as the war in the Pacific was coming to its eventual conclusion, American shipyards were churning out yet more *Essex*-class carriers. Pictured in July 1945 at the Philadelphia Navy Yard ready to be launched is the USS *Princeton* (CV-37), although it was not commissioned until November 1945. The Philadelphia Navy Yard was established in 1871 and continued until 1995. During the Second World War, its 40,000-strong workforce built fifty-three ships and repaired another 574. (*RWP*)

Following on the heels of the USS *Long Island* (CVE-1, originally AVG-1), appeared the four *Sangamon*-class escort carriers with the USS *Santee* (CVE-29) shown here. The letter suffix designation code 'CVE' stood for escort aircraft carrier and was applied in July 1943. Of all the CVEs commissioned by the US navy, the *Sangamon* class was the largest model built and the only class to operate dive-bombers during the Second World War. (*RWP*)

(*Above*) In one of only a few dozen colour photographs of Second World War US navy carriers, we see the pre-war-built USS *Saratoga* (CV-3), one of the two carriers of the *Lexington* class. It is shown here moored at Ford Island, Pearl Harbor in late May or early June 1942. The ship sports a solid dark blue colour intended to reduce the carrier's observability from the air. (*NA*)

(*Left*) Arranged on the flight deck of the wartime USS *Yorktown* (CV-10), an *Essex*-class carrier, is the bulk of its air group warming engines, ready to be launched. In the foreground are the fighters, with torpedo-bombers behind the fighters and dive-bombers at the very rear portion of the flight deck. By the later stages of the Second World War, as the kamikaze threat rose, there were as many as seventy-two fighters assigned to an *Essex*-class carrier. (*NA*)

Shown during its launching in September 1942 is the *Essex*-class carrier USS *Lexington* (CV-16). Notice the ship has not yet been fitted with its island. The two tugs seen in the picture will push the ship to a fitting-out dock where it will be completed. It was commissioned on 17 February 1943 and remained in service with the US navy until late 1991, before its final decommissioning. *(NA)*

The last *Essex*-class carrier completed for the US navy was the USS *Oriskany* (CV-34). It was launched on 13 October 1945 but not commissioned until 25 September 1950 as there were already too many *Essex*-class carriers in service in the immediate aftermath of the Second World War. The ship was decommissioned in 1976 and scuttled, as shown here, on 17 May 2006 in the Gulf of Mexico as an artificial reef. *(DOD)*

A Grumman TBF Avenger torpedo-bomber is being brought up to the flight deck of the USS *Santee* (CVE-29) by the ship's centreline elevator during the Second World War. The ship was one of four carriers in the *Sangamon* class and was commissioned on 25 August 1942. The ship was sold for scrap in March 1959. (*NA*)

From the stern of the flight deck of the USS *Santee* looking forward on the port side of the ship can be seen a number of Douglas SBD-3 Dauntless dive-bombers. On the starboard side of the carrier's flight deck can be seen Grumman F4F-4 Wildcat fighters with wings folded. This photograph was taken during Operation TORCH, the Allied invasion of Vichy French North Africa, in November 1942. (*NA*)

In this picture dated 27 October 1945 we see the USS *Franklin D. Roosevelt* (CVB-42) during its commissioning ceremony. The carrier was the second ship in the *Midway* class. Notice the numerous 5-inch gun turrets just below the ship's flight deck on its port side. At the stern of the ship can be seen 20mm anti-aircraft guns on the upper level and quad 40mm anti-aircraft guns on the lower level. *(NA)*

A picture taken from the island looking towards the stern portion of the flight deck of the USS *Essex* (CVA-9) following the conclusion of the Korean War. Coming up on one of the ship's two centreline elevators is a Grumman F9F-2 Panther, the first carrier-borne jet to see combat. On the rear of the carrier's flight deck is a rescue helicopter. *(NNAM)*

Pictured moored to a pier in 1962 is the USS *Ticonderoga* (CVA-14). The ship was launched on 7 February 1944 and commissioned on 8 May 1944. It saw action during the later stages of the Second World War. It missed the Korean War but saw action during the Vietnam conflict. The US navy decommissioned the carrier in 1973. *(NNAM)*

Tugs are shown pushing the USS *Midway* (CV-41) towards the navy pier in San Diego Harbor on 10 January 2004. It opened as a museum ship on 7 June that year. When commissioned on 10 September 1945 it was the largest US navy carrier built up to that time, was the first in the three ships of the *Midway* class and the only example preserved. It lasted in US navy service until being decommissioned on 11 April 1992. *(DOD)*

(*Above*) The USS *Saratoga* (CVA-60), the second in the four ships that made up the *Forrestal* class of carriers, is shown sailing alongside the replenishment oiler USS *Kalamazoo* (AOR-6). The *Forrestal* class of carriers was the replacement for the three *Midway*-class carriers. The USS *Saratoga* was commissioned on 14 April 1956 and decommissioned in 1994. (*DOD*)

(*Right*) Commissioned on 27 October 1961 was the USS *Constellation* (CVA-64) seen here, the second ship in the four carriers of the *Kitty Hawk* class which were the follow-on to the four *Forrestal*-class carriers. During its construction in 1960 the USS *Constellation* suffered a serious fire that resulted in $75 million worth of damage to the carrier. (*DOD*)

In a picture from 1994 the USS *Enterprise* (CVN-65) is shown at Newport News Shipyard, Virginia where it had been undergoing a four-year overhaul and nuclear reactor re-coring. The large letter 'E' painted on the ship's island reflects its popular nickname of the 'Big E'. It was the first nuclear-powered carrier constructed for the US navy. *(DOD)*

The first ship in the ten-ship class of *Nimitz* carriers was the USS *Nimitz* (CVN-68), seen here in 2013. To improve the carrier's ability to defend itself from aerial threats, the USS *Nimitz* and two other carriers in its class have been fitted with an integrated battle management system designed and built by Raytheon, known as the Ship Self-Defense System (SSDS). *(DOD)*

(*Right*) Despite the incredible array of sophisticated technology that has gone into the design of the *Nimitz*-class supercarriers, without the sweat and toil of hardworking young men and women such as the flight deck crewman pictured, the carriers would never sail. Typically, just a bit less than half the 6,000 personnel on board a *Nimitz*-class carrier are part of the air wing assigned to the ship. The remaining members are responsible for the operation of the vessel. (*DOD*)

(*Below*) An artist's interpretation of the USS *Gerald R. Ford* (CVN-78) following completion, which is planned for 2016. It will be the first ship in a class of new carriers referred to as the *Gerald R. Ford* or *Ford* class intended to eventually replace the *Nimitz*-class carriers. To reduce the cost of operating this new class of carriers, a great deal of automation has gone into the ship's design in order to reduce manning requirements. (*DOD*)

In the same general mould as the USS *Long Island* was the USS *Charger* (CVE-30), shown here in May 1942. The carrier was the sole ship in its class and never saw combat: rather, it was employed throughout the Second World War as a training ship by the US navy. Despite its wartime training role, it was armed with a number of anti-aircraft guns. (*RWP*)

Between September 1942 and April 1943 the US navy took into service eleven CVEs, referred to as the *Bogue* class. Pictured on 1 July 1943 in the Pacific is the USS *Barnes* (CVE-20) in the aircraft transport role, with US Army Air Force twin-engine Lockheed P-38 Lightning fighters and single-engine Republic P-47 Thunderbolt fighters stored on its flight deck. (*RWP*)

(*Above*) An August 1942 picture taken from the foremast of USS *Copahee* (CVE-12) looking down into the open top of the ship's navigation bridge. While the *Copahee* was employed as an aircraft transport ship during the Second World War, other ships in its class saw useful service in the anti-submarine warfare (ASW) role. (*RWP*)

(*Opposite above*) There were no large crash and salvage cranes on Second World War-era US navy CVEs. When there was a problem with a plane that could not be moved by a flight deck taxi, it fell to raw muscle power to rectify matters. Here we see those muscles in action on the USS *Bogue* (CVE-9) in June 1944 with the ship's crew attempting to haul a General Motors-built TBM Avenger torpedo-bomber back onto the flight deck. (*NA*)

(*Opposite below*) A stern view of the USS *Copahee* (CVE-12) pictured in a dazzle-painted camouflage scheme. It was commissioned into US navy service in June 1942 and spent its wartime career as an aircraft transport ship. The vessel had a crew of 890 officers and enlisted personnel. Its fuel oil-fired boilers powered steam turbine engines that gave it and its sister ships a top speed of 16.6 knots. (*RWP*)

(*Above*) The largest class of CVEs employed by the US navy during the Second World War proved to be the fifty ships of the *Casablanca* class. Pictured is the USS *Matanikau* (CVE-101), commissioned in June 1944, it served as an aircraft transport ship and a training ship for pilots during its wartime service. It had a crew complement of 860 men. (*NNAM*)

(*Opposite page*) This overhead view shows a large variety of aircraft stored on the flight deck of the USS *Thetis Bay* (CVE-90), a *Casablanca*-class escort carrier. Visible are eight Consolidated PBY Catalina patrol flying boats, a single Grumman J2F Duck biplane and eighteen additional Grumman F6F Hellcats with wings folded. The ship was commissioned in April 1944 and was an aircraft transport ship throughout the Second World War. (*NNAM*)

(*Below*) The successful launch and recovery of aircraft on board carriers has always been a very labour-intensive job. This wartime picture taken on board a US navy CVE shows the multitude of personnel needed to place just a single plane into the air. Everybody in this photograph had a vital job that needed to be performed at the right time and in the right manner. Any deviation from the standard routines could result in death or dismemberment. (*NA*)

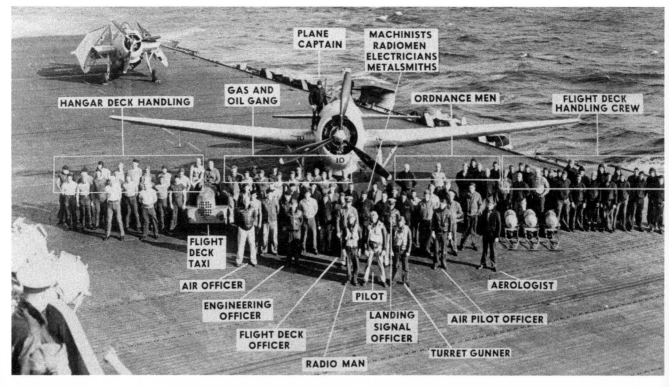

U.S.S. SALERNO
CVE 110
Broad on Port Bow
JUNE 3, 1945

The last class of CVEs taken into service by the US navy during the Second World War was the *Commencement Bay* class. Pictured is the USS *Salerno Bay* (CVE-110) in 1945. Based on converted tankers, the *Commencement Bay* class of CVEs were commissioned too late in the war to see much action, with some being cancelled as the worldwide conflict came to an end. (*RWP*)

To allow new pilots the opportunity to acquire the important skills needed to both successfully launch and recover off carrier flight decks and not to burden the existing carrier inventory with the job, the US navy bought two former Great Lake paddle-wheel passenger steamers in 1942. They were modified to accommodate a 550 feet-long flight deck. The second one acquired was the USS *Sable* (IX-81) seen here. The 'IX' hull number stood for unclassified miscellaneous auxiliary. (*NNAM*)

Chapter Three

Post-War Aircraft Carriers

Following the Japanese surrender in September 1945, the US navy quickly disposed of its remaining pre-war fleet carriers. These included the USS *Saratoga* (CV-3), USS *Ranger* (CV-4) and USS *Enterprise* (CV-6), with the latter being decommissioned in February 1947.

Of the seventeen *Essex*-class carriers in service at the conclusion of the Second World War, there were only eight still in use by 1947 with the remaining ships decommissioned and placed in the inactive reserve fleet. The wartime-damaged USS *Franklin* (CV-13) and USS *Bunker Hill* (CV-17) were never recommissioned.

Those *Essex*-class carriers retained in service in the immediate post-war era included USS *Boxer* (CV-21), USS *Leyte* (CV-32), USS *Kearsarge* (CV-33), USS *Antietam* (CV-36), USS *Princeton* (CV-37), USS *Tarawa* (CV-40), USS *Valley Forge* (CV-45) and USS *Philippine Sea* (CV-47).

Essex-Class Post-War Upgrades

In June 1947 the US navy began a programme referred to as Project SCB-27A. This entailed the modernization of some of the *Essex*-class carriers, most then in the inactive reserve fleet. The purpose of this upgrade programme was to give the ships the capability to operate the larger, heavier jet aircraft that were entering into service.

The first *Essex*-class carrier selected for the Project SCB-27A upgrading process in August 1947 was the unfinished USS *Oriskany* (CV-34). It was followed by eight others of the *Essex* class: USS *Essex* (CV-9), USS *Yorktown* (CV-10), USS *Hornet* (CV-12), USS *Randolph* (CV-15), USS *Wasp* (CV-18), USS *Bennington* (CV-20), USS *Kearsarge* (CV-33) and USS *Lake Champlain* (CV-39).

There were a great many improvements made to the nine *Essex*-class carriers selected for Project SCB-27A. These included the fitting of the latest radars, an enlarged forward centreline elevator, installation of two sets of ballistic- and flame-proof doors on the armoured hangar deck and a strengthened flight deck.

Another big change for the carriers selected for this upgrading process was the relocation of the pilots' ready rooms (pre-flight briefing rooms). Rather than being located directly under the unarmoured flight deck in the galley deck, they were moved to the second deck, located under the armoured hangar deck. To ease the transit of the pilots from the second deck to the flight deck, an escalator was added to the starboard side of the ship's island, connecting the hangar deck to the flight deck.

A key identifying feature of all the post-war modernized *Essex*-class carriers under Project SCB-27A was the removal of the four armoured mounts armed with twin 5-inch/38 calibre dual-purpose guns, two forward of the ships' islands and two aft. Dual-purpose meant that the guns were capable of engaging both surface and aerial targets. Late-production *Essex*-class carriers had only two of these dual-purpose guns fitted, one forward of the island and one aft.

As the US navy new post-war carrier jets were much thirstier than the wartime prop-driven planes, Project SCB-27A also involved the fitting of larger aviation fuel tanks on board the nine *Essex*-class carriers selected for the programme. This was accomplished by doing away with the armour belt on either side of the carriers' hulls and extending their beam by 8 feet.

A Second Upgrading Project

Even as Project SCB-27A was progressing, new advancements in both carrier and carrier aircraft designs compelled the US navy to adjust its plans. It was decided that six additional unmodified *Essex*-class carriers would go through a new upgrading process, as well as the USS *Oriskany*, already upgraded under SCB-27A.

The previously unmodified *Essex*-class carriers to go through this new upgrade programme, labelled Project SCB-27C, included the USS *Intrepid* (CV-11), USS *Ticonderoga* (CV-14), USS *Lexington* (CV-16), USS *Hancock* (CV-19), USS *Bon Homme Richard* (CV-31) and USS *Shangri-La* (CV-38).

Project SCB-27C included the addition of a new more powerful British-designed steam catapult system and the removal of one of the carrier's two centreline elevators. The deleted aft (rear) near centreline elevator was replaced by another deck-edge elevator located aft of the carrier's islands on the starboard side. Another design change was an increase in the carrier's beam of 11 feet.

In October 1952 the US navy classified the majority of its modernized *Essex*-class carriers as 'attack carriers' and assigned them the new letter suffix designation code 'CVA'. The CVAs normally carried a combination of aircraft (i.e. fighters and fighter-bombers) and attack aircraft, assigned the letter suffix 'AD', the latter being capable of delivering nuclear weapons. Also carried on board the CVAs were special-purpose aircraft such as photo reconnaissance and airborne early warning planes, the first of the latter being the WF-1 Tracer.

The Angled Flight Deck Appears

The British wartime concept of the angled flight deck greatly enthralled the senior leadership of the post-war US navy. It allowed for the separation of the aircraft launching area of a carrier's flight deck from the aircraft recovery area, thus preventing recovering aircraft that missed the flight deck arresting gear from crashing into the aircraft stored or those preparing to go airborne from the flight deck launching area. As a secondary benefit, the fitting of an angled deck to a carrier also freed up a great deal of space in the middle of the flight deck for additional aircraft storage.

To test the merits of the angled flight deck, the US navy fitted the *Essex*-class USS *Antietam* (CVA-36) with an experimental angled flight deck in 1952. Test results were extremely promising and the US navy wasted no time in modifying three more *Essex*-class carriers with angled flight decks, under a programme referred to as Project SCB-125. These were the USS *Lexington* (CVA-16), USS *Bon Homme Richard* (CVA-31) and USS *Shangri-La* (CVA-38), which had all undergone the Project SCB-27C modernization process.

The first of the three carriers to be re-commissioned with the Project SCB-125 upgrade was the USS *Shangri-La* in 1955. The USS *Antietam* was never modernized under Project SCB-125, other than having been fitted with the experimental angled flight deck.

Other improvements to the three *Essex*-class carriers selected for upgrading under Project SCB-125 included the relocation of their primary flight control to the aft end of their islands. To supplement the human landing signal officer (LSO), the upgraded carriers were fitted with a Royal Navy-invented device known as the Mirror Optical Landing System (MOLS).

The first three *Essex*-class carriers modified under Project SCB-27C – the USS *Intrepid*, USS *Ticonderoga* and USS *Hancock* – were retro-fitted with angled flight decks to conform to the Project SCB-125 standard in 1957. In addition, eight of the nine *Essex*-class carriers that had previously received the Project SCB-27A upgrades were fitted with angled flight decks under Project SCB-125.

Of the various post-war modernization upgrades, only the USS *Oriskany* went through Project SCB-27A, Project SCB-27C and Project SCB-125 upgrades. The carrier was also the only *Essex*-class vessel to be fitted with an aluminium flight deck in place of the standard unarmoured metal flight deck covered with wooden planking.

Another design feature that appeared on the *Essex*-class carriers brought up to the Project SCB-125 standard was an enclosed hurricane bow in place of the original open bow space. As time went on, all the post-war modernized *Essex*-class carriers that went through Project SCB-27A and Project SCB-27C were retro-fitted with enclosed hurricane bows. All four surviving *Essex*-class carriers currently preserved as museum ships – USS *Yorktown* (CVS-10), USS *Intrepid* (CVS-11), USS *Hornet* (CVS-12) and USS *Lexington* (AVT-16) – were brought up to the Project SCB-125 standard.

The Submarine Threat

The Soviet navy began building and deploying a large number of submarines in the early 1950s. To meet this new Cold War threat, the US navy originally wanted to modify some of its remaining wartime CVEs for ASW (anti-submarine warfare) duties. The other recourse was to build a new class of CVEs designed specifically for that role. However, the funding for these programmes was never authorized. Therefore the back-up plan eventually involved converting nineteen of the modernized *Essex*-class carriers for this role. The first was converted in 1955 and the last in 1969. Those modified for this new job were assigned the letter suffix designation code 'CVS' that indicated ASW ships.

The End of the Road
The various modernization programmes implemented by the US navy beginning in the late 1940s did much to extend the service life of the *Essex*-class carriers. However, it was clear to the senior leadership that the useful lifespan of the ships was nearing an end. As early as 1957 US navy Admiral Arleigh Burke stated:

> We are limited by how far we can go in modernization by the age of the ships. They are getting old. Their machinery is wearing out and they are becoming progressively more expensive to maintain. Like an old car, they must be replaced.

The very first of the modernized *Essex*-class carriers to be decommissioned was the USS *Leyte* (CV-32) in 1959, with the majority being retired in the 1970s. The last of the *Essex* class to be decommissioned was the USS *Lexington* (CV-16) in 1991, which had been a training ship since 1963. It had been assigned the letter suffix designation code CVT in 1969 to better reflect its new role, the letter 'T' in the suffix standing for 'training'.

The USS *Antietam* (CVS-36) had been employed as a training ship from 1957 to 1962 prior to the USS *Lexington*. Some of the *Essex*-class carriers eventually spent time as aircraft transports before being retired. In such a role they were assigned the letter suffix designation code AVT, as was eventually the USS *Lexington* (originally CV-16).

Three of the eight unmodernized *Essex*-class carriers were eventually converted into amphibious assault ships between 1958 and 1961. These were the USS *Boxer* (CV-21), USS *Princeton* (CV-37) and USS *Valley Forge* (CV-45). In this new role they were assigned the letter suffix designation code 'LPH', standing for Landing Platform, Helicopter. Their new job entailed carrying transport helicopters to move Marines from ship to shore and back again. All three were retired from that role by 1971 as dedicated ships designed from the keel up for the purpose took their places.

The End for the Light Carriers
Of the US navy's nine wartime *Independence*-class carriers, eight survived the conflict. The USS *Monterey* (CVL-26) initially became a training carrier for pilots post-war. It later saw use as an AVT before being decommissioned in January 1956. The

USS *Cabot* (CVL-28) and the USS *Bataan* (CVL-29) spent some time post-war as ASW carriers before being decommissioned in the mid-1950s. The USS *San Jacinto* (CVL-30) was decommissioned in 1947. It was later reclassified as an AVT in the reserve fleet but never saw use in that role before being sold for scrapping in 1970.

The USS *Cabot* had a second career with the Spanish navy as SNS *Dedalo* (R01), beginning in 1967 and ending in 1989. The USS *Belleau Wood* (CVL-24) and the USS *Langley* (CVL-27) were both decommissioned in 1947. However, they had second careers with the French navy beginning in the early 1950s. They were returned to the US navy in the early 1960s and quickly sold for scrapping as they could not handle the larger jet aircraft then coming into service.

By mid-1944 the US navy had begun work on two new light carriers of an improved design. They were to be based on the enlarged hulls of *Baltimore*-class heavy cruisers. These were the USS *Saipan* (CVL-48) and the USS *Wright* (CVL-49) and both were commissioned following the Second World War. The ships were designated the *Saipan* class and had a full load displacement of 20,000 tons. They had an overall length of 683 feet 7 inches and carried fifty aircraft which were moved between decks by two centreline elevators and launched by two hydraulic catapults.

The *Saipan* class served as carriers until the mid-1950s. Following this employment, the two *Saipan*-class carriers went on to second careers with the USS *Saipan* becoming the USS *Arlington* (AGMR-2). The letter suffix code 'AGMR' designated it as a major communication relay ship. The USS *Wright* retained its original name but received a new letter suffix designation code 'CC' standing for command ship and became the USS *Wright* (CC-2). Both these ships survived in their new roles until they were pulled out of service in 1970 and sold for scrapping.

The End for the Escort Carriers

Of the various escort carrier classes taken into service by the US navy during the Second World War, the *Sangamon* class soon disappeared when the conflict ended, as did the sole *Charger*-class escort carrier. Some of the *Bogue*-class escort carriers survived into the post-war era with a bewildering number of different letter suffix designation codes. Starting with the wartime suffix designation code CVE, they then went on to become escort helicopter aircraft carriers (CVHEs), then utility carriers (CVUs) and finally aviation transports (AKUs) during the Vietnam War. Following that conflict they were retired and sold for scrapping.

The *Casablanca*-class escort carriers followed the same path as the *Bogue* class, with some retained post-war and eventually redesignated as CVHEs, later as CVUs and finally becoming AKUs. The majority of the *Bogue*-class escort carriers were decommissioned by 1959.

As an experiment the USS *Thetis Bay* (CVE-90), a *Casablanca*-class escort carrier, became an Assault Helicopter Aircraft Carrier (CVHA-1) in 1955. It was redesignated as Amphibious Assault Ship, Helicopter (LPH-6) in 1959. The experiment was not judged a success and no other *Casablanca*-class escort carriers were converted to the new role. The *Thetis Bay* had its final decommissioning in 1964.

Of the nineteen *Commencement Bay*-class escort carriers that were in service when the Second World War ended, seven of them were immediately pulled from service and eventually sold for scrapping. The remaining ships saw post-war service in a variety of roles, including anti-submarine support carriers (CVSs) and as auxiliary aircraft landing training ships (AVTs). Two of them were converted into AGMRs and lasted in service until 1970. The last of the *Commencement Bay*-class escort carriers that had been converted into CVSs were pulled from service in 1971 as they were not large enough to safely launch and recover the newest generation of ASW aircraft.

New Post-War Fleet Carriers

Early wartime combat experience had convinced the US navy that a new, larger fleet carrier reflecting the latest in ship design technology would be needed to supplement and eventually replace the *Essex*-class carriers, which reflected pre-war ship design technology. The next-generation fleet carrier would also need an armoured flight deck for added survivability.

The US navy's desire for an armoured flight deck came about due to the reports before America's official entry into the Second World War of the ability of Royal Navy carriers fitted with armoured flight decks to absorb a great deal of punishment in battle and continue to function. An added benefit in fitting the next generation of US navy fleet carriers with armoured flight decks would be their ability to bear the weight of the upcoming generations of larger and heavier carrier aircraft.

Congress authorized the building of six new fleet carriers in June 1942. They were to be designated the *Midway* class and assigned the letter suffix designation code 'CVB', with the letter 'B' standing for 'battle'. However, only the first three were built, all being commissioned following the end of the Second World War. These were the USS *Midway* (CVB-41), USS *Franklin D. Roosevelt* (CVB-42) and USS *Coral Sea* (CVB-43).

The *Midway*-class carriers had an overall length of 968 feet and a full load displacement of 55,000 tons. The ship's armoured flight deck was 3.5 inches thick and was considered part of the superstructure. Its hangar deck was considered the main deck, or strength deck, as it had been on the previous *Essex*-class carriers. The hangar deck on the *Midway* class was unarmoured to save weight.

The *Midway*-class carriers had been intended to carry as many as 144 aircraft that would be launched with the assistance of two hydraulically-operated flight deck catapults. As carrier aircraft became ever larger and heavier in the post-war years, the number of planes carried on board the ships dropped. At face value it might seem that the smaller number of aircraft would lessen the carrier's effectiveness but the newer generation of aircraft was much more capable than their predecessors, off-setting the decline in numbers. Planes on the ships were moved between the flight and hangar decks by two centreline and one port-side deck-edge elevator.

The USS *Franklin D. Roosevelt* was the initial US navy carrier modified to handle nuclear weapons in 1950. The first US navy aircraft able to carry a nuclear weapon and be launched from a *Midway*-class carrier was a modified land-based, twin-engine patrol aircraft designated the P2V. Twelve were modified for the role and designated the P2V-3C. Due to the size of the P2V-3C they were not intended to be recovered by the *Midway*-class carriers. They were a stopgap solution until the specially-designed AJ-1 Savage entered service, which occurred in late 1949. It was designed to be both launched and recovered from *Midway*-class carriers.

In 1952 the US navy redesignated the *Midway*-class carriers as CVAs rather than CVBs, the letter 'A' now standing for 'attack'. In 1975 the US navy redesignated the *Midway*-class carriers once again and they now became just CVs.

As with many of the *Essex*-class carriers, the three *Midway*-class carriers also went through modernization programmes, beginning in 1953 with the USS *Franklin D. Roosevelt*. The programmes were referred to as Project SCB-110 and Project SCB-110A and provided the ships with angled flight decks and other improvements such as an enclosed hurricane bow.

The first *Midway*-class carrier to return to service with the Project SCB-110 and Project SCB-110A upgrades was the USS *Franklin D. Roosevelt* in 1956, followed by the USS *Midway* in 1957 and the USS *Coral Sea* in 1960.

As the march of technology continued in naval aviation the *Midway*-class carriers, like those that went before them, were unable to operate the latest generation of larger and heavier carrier aircraft. By the 1970s, they were also just old and worn out and a massive conversion was not cost-effective. It was therefore decided to retire the three *Midway*-class carriers. The first to go was the *Franklin D. Roosevelt* in 1977, the *Coral Sea* in 1990 and the *Midway* in 1992, the latter having a second career as a museum ship berthed in San Diego Harbor since 2004.

A False Start

The next class of US navy post-war carriers was to be the four *United States*-class carriers, the first being approved by the acting secretary of the US navy in September 1947. The keel of the first in this class of new carriers, the USS *United States* (CVA-58), was laid down on 18 April 1949.

Due to fierce in-service disagreements between the US navy and the newly-formed US Air Force (formerly the US Army Air Force) on who was to be in charge of delivering America's arsenal of nuclear weapons in case of the outbreak of a third world war, the new carrier was cancelled five days later on 23 April by the new incoming pro-Air Force Secretary of Defense.

The cancelled USS *United States* was to have had an overall length of 1,090 feet with an estimated full load displacement of 83,200 tons. It would have been large enough to operate the US navy's proposed new carrier aircraft designed to deliver nuclear weapons, which then weighed in the multi-ton range. Since it was anticipated that the largest of these new nuclear-capable carrier aircraft would have a wingspan of up to 110 feet, the US navy's aviators had insisted that the USS *United States* be flush-decked, as was their first carrier, the USS *Langley* (CV-1).

In 1962 Secretary of Defense Robert S. McNamara took the responsibility of strategic nuclear attack away from the US navy's carrier inventory. That role was transferred to the US navy's nuclear-powered ballistic missile submarines (SSBNs) equipped with the nuclear-armed Polaris ballistic missile system and the US Air Force's inventory of land-based intercontinental ballistic missiles (ICBMs). Up till that point, the typical US navy carrier operated up to fifty aircraft capable of carrying the follow-on generation of smaller and lighter nuclear weapons.

The Second Time Around is the Charm

The future of US navy aircraft carriers in the immediate post-war years was secured by the sterling service during the Korean War of the *Essex*-class carriers that provided the majority of carrier-based air support throughout the conflict. Acting in supporting roles during the Korean War were a few *Independence*-class carriers and some of the US navy's remaining escort carriers. US navy carrier aircraft shot down fifty-one enemy planes during the Korean War, losing only five of their own to enemy aircraft. Another 559 US navy aircraft were lost to enemy anti-aircraft fire during the same conflict.

While officially referred to only as a police action, the Korean War showed that limited war was still possible in an age of nuclear weapons. It was now clear to America's political elite that carriers still had a critical role to play in the American military arsenal. This led to Congressional approval in July 1951 of the funding needed to build a new class of carriers referred to as the *Forrestal* class. It comprised four ships commissioned between 1955 and 1959: the USS *Forrestal* (CVA-59), USS *Saratoga* (CVA-60), USS *Ranger* (CVA-61) and USS *Independence* (CVA-62).

The *Forrestal*-class carriers had an overall length of 1,039 feet and a full load displacement of 76,600 tons. The first two ships in the class were originally intended to have been commissioned with axial flight decks but were redesigned while under construction for the fitting of angled flight decks. The last two *Forrestal*-class carriers were built from the keel up with angled flight decks.

The *Forrestal* class was the first to be designed from the keel up to operate jet-powered aircraft. It was also the first to be tagged with the unofficial but still popular term 'supercarrier' as the ships had a displacement over 65,000 tons.

The *Forrestal*-class carriers typically carried seventy-five aircraft, launched with the aid of four compressed-air and later steam-powered catapults. The planes were transported between the armoured flight deck and the unarmoured hangar deck by three starboard deck-edge elevators and a single port-side one, thereby making the *Forrestal*-class carriers the first in US navy service to do without centreline elevators from the beginning.

Unlike all the US navy carriers that preceded them, the flight deck on the *Forrestal*-class carriers was now the main deck (or strength deck). This design arrangement would be found on all subsequent classes of US navy carriers.

The US navy began pulling the *Forrestal*-class carriers out of service in the early 1990s, the first to be decommissioned being the USS *Ranger* in July 1993. It was followed by the decommissioning of the USS *Forrestal* in September 1993, the USS *Saratoga* in August 1994 and the USS *Independence* in September 1998. There had been plans to turn the *Forrestal* into a training carrier in 1992 but that was not to be.

Kitty Hawk-Class Carriers

US navy plans had originally called for the *Forrestal* class to consist of eight carriers. However, lessons learned in the building and operation of the first four resulted in a number of design changes being incorporated into the last three ships ordered. Reflecting these changes, the US navy decided to rename them the *Kitty Hawk* class. These were the USS *Kitty Hawk* (CVA-63), USS *Constellation* (CVA-64) and USS *America* (CVA-66). The first was commissioned in June 1961 and the last in September 1964.

Beginning in the early 1970s, the *Kitty Hawk*-class carriers were redesignated by the US navy from the letter suffix designation code CVA to simply CV. This was based on the new multi-purpose roles assigned to them, which included ASW duties. This had previously been performed by the modified *Essex*-class carriers that had been assigned the letter suffix designation code CVS. The *Kitty Hawk*-class carriers have also been referred to by some as the improved *Forrestal*-class carriers.

The *Kitty Hawk* class had an overall length of 1,062 feet 6 inches and a full load displacement of 80,880 tons. They typically carried seventy-five aircraft that were launched by four steam-powered catapults. The ships' planes were transported between the flight deck and hangar deck by four deck-edge elevators, as with the preceding *Forrestal*-class carriers.

Experience with the single port-side deck-edge elevator on the *Forrestal*-class carriers had shown that its location at the most forward portion of the angled flight deck resulted in operational problems as it was in the way of both launching and recovering aircraft. On the *Kitty Hawk* class the port-side deck-edge elevator was relocated to the rearmost portion of the angled flight deck and this design arrangement of elevators has remained the standard for all US navy carrier classes through to today's *Nimitz* class.

As the US navy had begun favouring nuclear-powered carriers in the 1950s, the *Kitty Hawk* class was eventually decommissioned. The first was the USS *America* in August 1996, followed by the USS *Constellation* in August 2002 and the last was the USS *Kitty Hawk* in January 2009.

Kennedy-Class Carrier

The USS *John F. Kennedy* (CV-67) can be seen as the last *Kitty Hawk*-class carrier constructed and featured a number of design improvements and changes from its three sister ships. It was officially labelled by the US navy as the single ship of the *John F. Kennedy* class, a subclass of the *Kitty Hawk* class.

The most prominent external differences between the first three *Kitty Hawk*-class carriers and the USS *John F. Kennedy* consisted of a slightly different design for its island and its angled stack that projected out over the starboard side of the ship. The previous *Kitty Hawk* carriers had a single straight stack. (In nautical terms a 'stack' is the pipe employed to expel exhaust smoke and gases away from the ship's boilers. The Royal Navy refers to them as 'funnels'.)

At one point in time, the US navy had planned that the USS *John F. Kennedy* would be nuclear-powered. However, that did not transpire and it would be the last conventionally-powered carrier built for the US navy. The USS *John F. Kennedy* was decommissioned in August 2007.

(*Opposite above*) Launched on 5 September 1945, three days after the Japanese surrender, was the USS *Philippine Sea* (CV-47) shown here in 1946, the same year it was commissioned. It featured the standard wartime array of four armoured mounts housing twin-5"/38 calibre dual-purpose guns. The ship was re-designated as a 'CVA' in 1952, with the letter 'A' standing for 'attack'. In 1955 the ship was designated as a 'CVS', with the letter 'S' representing its new role as a dedicated anti-submarine warfare (ASW) carrier. (*RWP*)

(*Opposite below*) Commissioned in April 1946 was the USS *Leyte* (CV-32), having been launched in August 1945. It, along with the other post-war *Essex*-class carriers, was re-designated as 'CVA' in 1952. It was converted into a dedicated anti-submarine carrier the following year and became a 'CVS'. (*RWP*)

The USS *Oriskany* (CV-34) seen here was the last *Essex*-class carrier authorized. The ship was launched in October 1945 but construction was suspended in 1947. Construction was eventually restarted and the carrier was finally commissioned in September 1950. In 1952 it became a 'CVA', a designation it retained until 1976 when it returned to the designation 'CV'. *(RWP)*

The first rescue/utility helicopter seen on post-war US navy carriers such as the *Essex* class was the Sikorsky HO3S-1. An example is seen here in 1952 being directed to a landing on board a carrier flight deck by an LSO (landing signal officer). The helicopter had a single pilot and could carry two or three lightly-equipped passengers. *(NNAM)*

Shown alongside a US navy replenishment ship is the USS *Philippine Sea* (CVS-47) with ASW aircraft and helicopters on the flight deck. The concept of replenishment at sea by the US navy was pioneered by Fleet Admiral Chester W. Nimitz prior to the Japanese attack at Pearl Harbor and was a key factor in operations during the Second World War. *(RWP)*

Not every aircraft designed for the US navy carrier service made the grade. One of these was the Ryan Aeronautical FR-1 Fireball, which was powered by both a prop-driven engine and a jet engine. The aircraft entered service in the last year of the Second World War but arrived too late to see combat. Immediate post-war use of the plane showed it to be too fragile to withstand the launch and recovery cycles on board carriers and it was pulled from front-line service by 1947. *(NNAM)*

(*Above*) As part of the Project SCB-125 upgrade, a number of post-war *Essex*-class carriers had angled flight decks fitted, as seen here on the USS *Hornet* (CVS-12). The ship is seen with one of the previous Project SCB-27C upgrades, which was the deletion of the carrier's aft near centreline elevator and its replacement with an aft deck-edge elevator behind the island. In this photograph the aft deck-edge elevator is in its stored vertical position. (*NNAM*)

(*Opposite page*) The USS *Yorktown* (CVA-10) is seen here in this post-war photograph with both the Project SCB-27A and Project SCB-125 upgrades that it received in 1955, including an angled flight deck and enclosed hurricane bow. After its wartime service, the ship was decommissioned in January 1947 and placed in storage. It was recommissioned in June 1952 but missed the Korean War. It was re-designated as a CVS in 1957 and then decommissioned for the final time in June 1970, becoming a museum ship. (*NNAM*)

Pictured is the post-war USS *Wasp* (CVA-18) with the Project SCB-27A upgrade, represented by the aft starboard-side deck-edge elevator. The Project SCB-125 upgrade to the carrier is shown by the angled flight deck and enclosed hurricane bow. On the flight deck of the carrier there appears a single Piasecki HUP-2 helicopter and a number of Grumman F9F-5 Panther fighters. (*RWP*)

One of the upgrades to the post-war *Essex*-class carriers under Project SCB-125 was the Mirror Optical Landing System (MOLS), an example of which is seen here on the starboard side of the USS *Antietam* (CVS-36) flight deck in 1961 with a Grumman S2F Tracker approaching. It worked on the principle of an approaching pilot making his own landing corrections by seeing the reflection of his aircraft in a large, stabilized mirror. The MOLS did not replace the wartime LSO but supplemented him. (*NNAM*)

By the 1960s the US navy had decided to replace the MOLS with another device known as the Fresnel Lens Optical Landing System (FLOLS), seen here. Pilots, and everybody else on carriers, call it the 'meatball' or just the 'ball'. It guides approaching pilots to a safe landing by using coloured Fresnel lenses. *(DOD)*

A view taken from a pilot's perspective as he approached the angled flight deck of the post-war USS *Essex* (CVS-9) with a nylon safety-net barrier erected on the flight deck. Prior to the adoption of the nylon safety-net barrier in the post-war era, US navy carriers employed wire barriers that were raised by crewmen if a prop-driven plane failed to catch any of the flight-deck arresting cables. *(RWP)*

U.S.S. LAKE CHAMPLAIN (CV39)
GENERAL VIEW AMIDSHIPS STBD.
N N S B.D.D. CO.

(*Above*) Shown at a shipyard in 1951 being upgraded with the Project SCB-27 improvements is the *Essex*-class carrier USS *Lake Champlain* (CV-39). It never had the Project SCB-125 upgrades that included an angled flight deck. The ship was commissioned in June 1945 but did not see combat during the Second World War. It left the shipyard in September 1952 and was re-designated as a CVA. In 1957 the carrier was designated as a CVS, the 'S' in the letter suffix designation code meaning that it was an ASW carrier. (*RWP*)

(*Opposite above*) Here we see a US navy Grumman F9F-5 Panther fighter that has been halted just before running into the nylon safety-net barrier erected on the post-war USS *Essex* (CVA-9). The adoption of the nylon net on board post-war US navy carriers proved a much-needed necessity as the wartime wire barriers tended to ride up the smooth noses of the newly-introduced jet-powered aircraft and fail to bring them to a halt. (*RWP*)

(*Opposite below*) The *Essex*-class carrier USS *Kearsarge* (CVA-33) is seen in this post-war photograph dated 1958. It was commissioned too late to see combat in the Second World War. However, it did go through both the Project SCB-27C and Project SCB-125 upgrades and was eventually designated a CVS in 1958. The four large straight-wing, twin-engine, prop/jet-driven aircraft seen on the carrier's flight deck are North American AJ-1 Savage long-range strategic bombers. (*RWP*)

(*Above*) The North American AJ-1 Savage long-range strategic bomber shown here was the US navy's first carrier-launched and carrier-recoverable aircraft able to deliver nuclear weapons. The three-man plane was first delivered to the fleet in 1949. Besides its two large prop-driven engines, it was also fitted with turbojet engine in its rear fuselage for take-off and burst speed as it had no defensive armament fitted. (*NNAM*)

(*Opposite above*) Shown being launched from the flight deck, with the assistance of a catapult, of the post-war USS *Shangri-La* (CVA-38) is a Douglas A-3 Skywarrior long-range strategic bomber. The jet-powered Skywarrior was the nuclear-armed replacement for the prop/jet-driven North American AJ-1 Savage. The USS *Shangri-La* had both the Project SCB-27C and Project SCB-125 upgrades, as is evident from the angled flight deck and hurricane bow. The ship was designated as a CVS in 1957. (*NNAM*)

(*Opposite below*) Preparing to take off from the flight deck of the *Essex*-class carrier USS *Antietam* (CV-36) during the Korean War are Chance-Vought F4U Corsair fighters. The Corsair was one of the few prop-driven aircraft to see combat in both the Second World War and the Korean War. The plane lasted in US navy service until 1955 and was also flown by the US Marine Corps. (*NNAM*)

Another aircraft to fly from *Essex*-class carriers during the Korean War and later, the Vietnam War, was the prop-driven, single-seat Douglas A-1 Skyraider seen here. The aircraft first entered service with the US navy in 1946 and lasted until 1972. It came in twenty-two different variants and in total, Douglas built 3,180 units of the Skyraider. *(RWP)*

Sometime during the Korean War, ordnance men aboard the *Essex*-class carrier USS *Philippine Sea* (CV-47) are shown below deck preparing bombs for delivery to the flight deck. All weapons aboard a carrier, from bombs to rockets, are under the supervision of the ordnance crew, also known as the 'bomb handlers'. Another popular nickname for the ordnance crew includes 'BB stackers'. *(RWP)*

A few of the *Essex*-class carriers never received the Project SCB-27A or Project SCB-125 upgrades. These included the USS *Boxer* (CVA-21), seen here in 1948. The tell-tale signs of no post-war upgrade include the 5"/38 calibre dual-purpose twin mounts seen just forward of the ship's island and the quad radar-equipped 40mm mount behind and above it. The aircraft on the flight deck is a North American FJ-1 Fury fighter. *(RWP)*

Another post-war *Essex*-class carrier that was never upgraded by the US navy under Project SCB-27A or SCB-125 was the USS *Princeton* (CVA-37). It, like so many other *Essex*-class carriers, was re-designated as a CVS in 1954. The last role it performed, beginning in 1959, was as a Landing Platform Helicopter (LPH) carrier. It is seen here with a large number of US Marine Corps Sikorsky UH-34D Seahorse troop-carrying helicopters on its flight deck. *(NNAM)*

The USS *Monterey* (CVL-26), an *Independence*-class light aircraft carrier, spent a few years following the Second World War as a training ship for pilots to hone their skills, both in being launched and recovered from carrier flight decks. This dramatic picture taken in 1953 shows how badly a carrier-landing could go wrong. The plane in the photograph is a North American SNJ-5 Texan, a two-man training aircraft. (*NNAM*)

Taking the lead from the building of the *Independence*-class carriers upon the hulls of *Cleveland*-class light cruisers, the US navy decided to have two additional light carriers constructed, named the *Saipan* class. They were based on the larger hulls and power plants of *Baltimore*-class heavy cruisers. The USS *Saipan* (CVL-48), pictured here in 1956, was launched in July 1945 but not commissioned until July 1946. *(RWP)*

The second ship in the *Saipan* class of light carriers was the USS *Wright* (CVL-49), shown here. It was launched in September 1945 and commissioned in February 1947. Like all the Second World War US navy carrier classes, it had hydraulic (oil-pneumatic) catapults. A large hydraulically-operated piston yanked a wire cable arrangement through a series of below-deck pulleys. The wire cable pulled on a flight-deck attachment referred to as a 'shuttle', to which the launching aircraft was attached, and hurled it into the sky. *(RWP)*

(*Above*) The USS *Rendova* (CVE-114) was a *Commencement Bay*-class escort carrier. It is seen here in this 1952 picture with Chance-Vought F4U Corsair fighters on its flight deck. The ship was launched in December 1944 and commissioned in October 1945, too late to see employment during the Second World War. However, it did see combat service during the Korean War. In 1959 the carrier was re-designated as an aviation transport ship (AKU) and saw its final decommissioning in 1971. (*RWP*)

(*Opposite above*) In a picture dated 1950 we can compare the respective sizes of the USS *Leyte* (CV-32), an *Essex*-class carrier on the right of the picture, and the USS *Wright* (CVL-49), a *Saipan*-class carrier on the left. The USS *Leyte* was among eight *Essex*-class carriers that never went through the Project SCB-27A and SCB-125 upgrades and were therefore never fitted with an angled flight deck. (*NNAM*)

(*Opposite below*) Acting as an aircraft transport ship in 1953 is the USS *Windham Bay* (CVE-92), one of the fifty *Casablanca*-class carriers built during the Second World War by the shipyards of American industrialist Henry J. Kaiser. The USS *Windham Bay* made numerous trips between the United States and South Korea during the Korean War, ferrying planes between the two nations. In 1955 the ship was re-designated as a utility aircraft carrier (CVU) and had its final decommissioning in 1959. (*RWP*)

(*Above*) This 1955 picture shows the USS *Point Cruz* (CVE-119), a *Commencement Bay*-class escort carrier acting as an ASW ship. On the forward flight deck is a rescue/utility helicopter. In 1957 it was designated as an AKU. In 1965 it was transferred to the civilian-operated Military Sea Transportation Service (MSTS) and was re-designated and re-numbered as the T-AKV-19. The ship had its final decommissioning in 1969. (*RWP*)

(*Opposite page*) In this photograph dated 1948, crew members of the USS *Badoeng Strait* (CVE-116) are engaged in target practice with their twin 40mm anti-aircraft gun mounts. The ship was a *Commencement Bay*-class escort carrier that was commissioned in February 1945. It was re-designated as an escort helicopter aircraft carrier (CHVE) in 1955 and a cargo ship/aircraft ferry (AKV) in 1959. The ship had its final decommissioning in 1970. (*RWP*)

(*Left*) A General Motors-built TBM Avenger pilot engaged in ASW work has managed to park his aircraft on the island of the USS *Siboney* (CVE-112) in this 1949 picture. One can only imagine the scramble that took place among the ship's personnel manning the open-topped flight control centre on the rear of the island as the plane came their way. The ship was a *Commencement Bay*-class carrier, became an AKV in 1959 and had its final decommissioning in 1970. (*NNAM*)

(*Opposite page*) On the heels of Congress authorizing the building of the first three *Essex*-class carriers, they went ahead and authorized in June 1942 the next generation of US navy carriers, referred to as the *Midway* class. This next-generation carrier class had an armoured flight deck copied from the Royal Navy, a first for the US navy. Pictured is the first ship in the class, the USS *Midway* (CVB-41). (*RWP*)

(*Below*) The year is 1958 and the ship is the USS *Thetis Bay* (CVE-90), originally a *Casablanca*-class carrier. Launched in March 1944, it was commissioned in April 1944. It was employed as an aircraft transport ship during the Second World War and designated a CVE but never saw combat. In 1955 it became CVHA-1, which lasted until 1959 when it was re-designated as LPH-6. The ship had its final decommissioning in 1964. (*RWP*)

(*Above*) On the flight deck of the USS *Midway*, four North American AJ-1 Savage long-range strategic bombers await their catapult launching. On the three *Midway*-class carriers there were originally eighteen dual-purpose 5"/54 calibre guns in single-gun armoured mounts. These were arranged along the ship's hangar-deck level with nine on either side of the ship's hull, some of which can be seen in this picture. This number was reduced as time went on and jet speeds rendered anti-aircraft guns less effective. (*NA*)

(*Opposite above*) During the many years that the USS *Midway* saw service, it operated a wide array of aircraft. One of the most unusual-looking was the Vought F7U Cutlass fighter shown here on the ship's flight deck in 1951. Development of the aircraft had begun in 1945, with its first carrier deployment in 1955. As the plane proved underpowered and had a large number of mechanical problems, it was not well-liked by those who flew or maintained it. The aircraft was pulled from service in 1957. (*NNAM*)

(*Opposite below*) As with many of the post-war *Essex*-class carriers, the three *Midway*-class vessels were eventually upgraded with angled flight decks as seen here in this picture of the USS *Midway*. The ships had their angled flight decks added under Project SCB-110, which also included improved elevators and a hurricane bow. With the angled flight decks, the carriers lost some of their port-side dual-purpose 5"/54 calibre guns. (*RWP*)

(*Above*) To prove that its carriers still had a role to play if a third world war occurred and not being able to wait for the delivery of a specialist-designed, long-distance, nuclear-capable bomber, the US navy decided to modify a small number of a new-model land-based maritime patrol plane. This was the Lockheed P2V Neptune, seen here, which was turned into a stopgap nuclear-capable bomber that could be operated off the flight deck of the navy's three new *Midway*-class carriers. In that new role, the aircraft was designated the P2V-3C. (*NNAM*)

(*Opposite above*) Shown in its original configuration with an axial flight deck is the USS *Franklin D. Roosevelt* (CVB-42), one of the three *Midway*-class carriers. The dual-purpose 5"/54 calibre guns in single armoured mounts on either side of the hulls of all three *Midway*-class carriers could fire a 70lb projectile out to a maximum effective range of 25,909 yards or up to a ceiling of 16,233 yards. (*RWP*)

(*Opposite below*) An aircraft seen in the early post-war years on US navy carriers was the Grumman F8F-1 Bearcat fighter shown here. It was the replacement for the Grumman F4F Wildcat and F6F Hellcat fighters employed during the Second World War. Initial design work began on the plane in 1943 but it showed up too late to see wartime service. The Bearcat disappeared from US navy service by 1953 as jet aircraft came to the forefront. (*RWP*)

(*Above*) A pilot's view coming in for a landing on the USS *Coral Sea*, with the LSO with his paddles seen on the very aft end of the flight deck, port-side. Note that the carrier's nylon safety net has been raised. If the LSO determined that an incoming aircraft had not met the correct landing parameters, the pilot was given a wave-off signal. If this occurred, the approaching pilot would then be forced to add power, climb back into the landing pattern and fly around for another attempt. (*NNAM*)

(*Opposite above*) One of the best-known jet-powered fighters to serve on the *Midway*-class carriers during their long careers was the McDonnell Douglas F-4 Phantom II. An example is seen here landing on the flight deck of the USS *Franklin D. Roosevelt*. It was originally designed as a high-altitude interceptor against Soviet bombers but eventually proved itself capable of other roles such as strike, suppression of enemy air defences and reconnaissance. (*NNAM*)

(*Opposite below*) Pictured in its original configuration is the USS *Coral Sea* (CVB-43) with an axial flight deck. The ship was commissioned with only fourteen of the 5″/54 calibre dual-purpose guns in single armoured mounts, rather than the eighteen fitted to the other two *Midway*-class carriers. As time went on, the carrier quickly lost its wartime 20mm and 40mm anti-aircraft guns. They were replaced with the post-war twin semi-automatic 3″/50 calibre dual-purpose guns that were fitted on unprotected pedestal mounts. (*NNAM*)

(*Right*) Parked on the flight deck of the USS *Coral Sea* is a McDonnell F3H Demon fighter. In 1962 during a major re-designation involving all the various services, it became the F-3 series. It served on US navy carriers beginning in 1956 and remained in service until 1964. The Demon was considered underpowered and was never a popular aircraft among those who flew them. It was replaced by the McDonnell Douglas F-4 Phantom II. (*NNAM*)

(*Opposite page*) As with all the *Midway*-class carriers, the USS *Coral Sea* went through an upgrading process during its long service life, which included the addition of an angled flight deck as seen in this 1979 picture. Another important feature of the upgrading process included the replacement of the ship's original elevators – two centreline and one deck-edge – with three new, larger deck-edge elevators; two on the starboard side of the carrier and one port-side. (*NNAM*)

The Northrop Grumman E-2 Hawkeye shown here in a picture dated 1970 belonged to an air wing then assigned to the USS *Coral Sea*. It is an airborne early warning (AEW) aircraft that began appearing on *Midway*-class carriers in the 1960s, with much-improved versions remaining in service today. It was the service's first purpose-built AEW plane. (*NNAM*)

(Above) An artist's conception of the proposed US navy supercarrier, *United States*, released in October 1948. Note the lack of an island and the introduction of four widely-spaced catapults, one on the starboard side in lieu of an island. With no place to install the various electronic sensors, plans had called for supporting ships in a carrier task force to feed the critical electronic data to the proposed *United States*. (NA)

(Opposite page) The USS *Forrestal* (CVA-59) shown here was the first US navy carrier built from the keel up with an angled flight deck. Previous carrier classes such as the *Essex* and *Midway* had their angled flight decks retro-fitted to the ships. It was also the first US navy carrier to be fitted with steam-powered catapults; a feature later retro-fitted to earlier classes of carriers. (NNAM)

(Right) Pictured is the laying of the 15-ton keel plate of the *United States* on 18 April 1949 at the Newport News Shipyard, Virginia. This caused an extremely negative reaction from the senior leadership of the United States Air Force who were convinced that the navy had designs on its mission of strategic air warfare and resulted in the carrier being cancelled a few days later. (Maritime Quest)

This picture shows the size comparison between the USS *Forrestal* on the right, a *Forrestal*-class carrier, and the USS *Intrepid* (CVA-11), a modernized *Essex*-class carrier with an angled flight deck, seen on the left. The USS *Forrestal* suffered two large accidental fires, the worst of which occurred in 1967 and killed 134 crewmen and wounded another 161. The same fire also destroyed twenty-one aircraft. *(NNAM)*

The USS *Saratoga* (CVA-60), seen here, was the second ship authorized in the *Forrestal* class of four carriers. Like the USS *Forrestal*, it was originally designed to have an axial flight deck but before being completed the plans were redrawn for the ship to include an angled flight deck. Defence from aerial and surface attack originally came from eight 5″/54 calibre guns in single armoured mounts, four on either side of the ship's hull, below flight-deck level. *(NNAM)*

On one of the four deck-edge elevators of the USS *Saratoga* can be seen a couple of Vought A-7 Corsair II attack aircraft. Intended as a successor to the McDonnell Douglas A-4 Skyhawk, the Corsair II entered service on US navy carriers in 1967 and went straight into action during the Vietnam War. Much-improved versions of the aircraft remained in US navy service until 1991. (*NNAM*)

Anchored off the Hawaiian island of Oahu with Diamond Head in the background is the USS *Ranger* (CVA-61), the third ship authorized in the *Forrestal* class of carriers. The ship's original eight dual-purpose 5″/54 calibre guns were eventually removed and replaced by the Raytheon Sea Sparrow Missile System and the General Dynamics Phalanx Close-in Weapon System (CIWS). (*NNAM*)

(*Above*) Undergoing modernization at a shipyard is the USS *Independence* (CVA-62), shown at the top of the picture, the last *Forrestal*-class carrier authorized. In the foreground of the picture is the much smaller pre-war USS *Enterprise* (CV-6) in storage, awaiting the chance to be saved from scrapping by becoming a museum ship. Like the USS *Ranger*, the USS *Independence* served during the Vietnam War. (*NNAM*)

(*Opposite page*) The forward portion of the island on the USS *Independence* is shown here. As with all late wartime and post-war US navy carrier classes, the island roof was dominated by a wide variety of electronic sensors. The uppermost windowed floor on the island is the 'navigation bridge' from which the carrier's commanding officer directs the ship's actions. The bottom windowed floor is known as the 'flag bridge' from which an admiral oversees a carrier strike group (CSG). (*NNAM*)

Returning to the Philadelphia Naval Shipyard upon completion of some of its sea trials prior to its commissioning is the USS *Kitty Hawk* (CVA-63), the first carrier authorized in the *Kitty Hawk* class. Note in this picture that the ship's foremast has been lowered to allow it to pass under bridges upon return to the shipyard. *(NNAM)*

A stern view of the USS *Kitty Hawk* showing off its extremely broad beam, common to all post-war carriers and a design trait required to preserve stability at sea. Such hulls require much more power to push through the sea than those with a narrow beam. Yet, the ability of a carrier to operate at high speed is crucial for success in launching its aircraft, since it must compensate for the shortness of its runway by travelling at high speed to produce wind for increased aircraft lift. *(DOD)*

The USS *Constellation* (CVA-64), shown here entering San Diego Harbor with its crew manning the rails in their dress white uniforms, was the second ship authorized in the *Kitty Hawk* class of carriers. The high speed required of all US navy carriers, both in wartime and then post-war prior to the introduction of nuclear-powered ships, was provided by fuel oil-fired boilers. *(DOD)*

Being guided to the catapult by a flight-deck crewman on the USS *Constellation* is a Grumman F-14 Tomcat two-seat fighter with its arresting hook down. The F-14 Tomcat assumed the role once performed by the McDonnell Douglas F-4 Phantom II. However, due to its large size, the F-14 Tomcat could not operate from the previous *Forrestal*-class carriers. *(DOD)*

(*Above*) The third ship authorized in the *Kitty Hawk* class was the USS *America* (CVA-66) seen here. During its long career it would see three deployments during the Vietnam War, take part in the April 1986 attack on Libyan military sites and see action during Operation DESERT STORM, the war on Iraq in 1991. (*DOD*)

(*Opposite above*) Within the Combat Information Center of the USS *America* in the 1980s, a sailor monitors his radar screen. It falls to the CIC watch officer to relieve radar operators at least every thirty minutes to prevent eye strain and fatigue. CICs were automated within US navy warships in the 1960s, reflecting the faster reaction times needed to deal with new post-war threats such as anti-ship cruise missiles. (*DOD*)

(*Opposite below*) The last ship authorized in the *Kitty Hawk* class of carriers was the USS *John F. Kennedy* (CVA-67). Due to the ever-increasing numbers of electronic sensors that the *Kitty Hawk* class of carriers were required to carry, a separate free-standing main mast located aft of the ship's island was installed, as seen here in this stern view of the USS *John F. Kennedy*. This was not a feature seen on the preceding *Forrestal* class. (*DOD*)

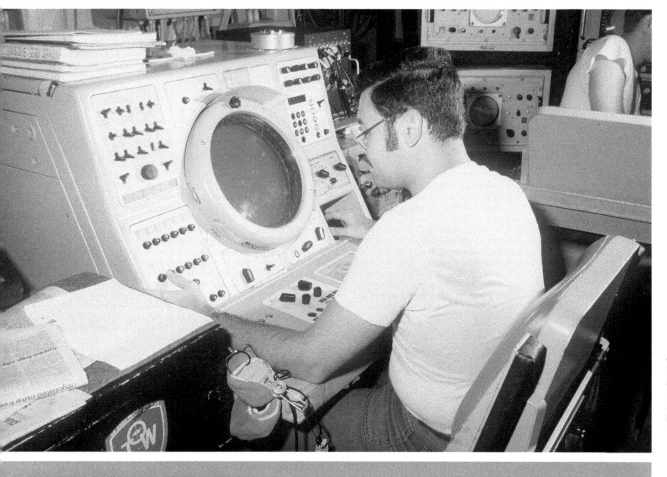

The first three ships in the *Kitty Hawk* class of carriers – USS *Kitty Hawk*, USS *Constellation* and USS *America* – were originally equipped with the RIM-2 Terrier surface-to-air missile. Pictured are two Terrier missiles on their launching unit. The Terrier missile system was removed from the *Kitty Hawk*-class carriers in the late 1970s. *(DOD)*

A picture from the 1970s shows the starboard side of the island on USS *America* (CVA-66). Projecting vertically from midway up the carrier's island is the supporting structure and the black antenna of the SPG-55 director radar for the RIM-2 Terrier surface-to-air missile. On top of the mast behind the island is an SPS-30 height-finding radar antenna. *(DOD)*

Chapter Four

Nuclear-Powered Aircraft Carriers

The idea for a nuclear-powered carrier had been under consideration by the US navy since early 1949. By 1952 Secretary of the Navy Dan A. Kimball said that he hoped the next carrier would be nuclear-powered. The Atomic Energy Commission and the Department of Defense (DOD) jointly announced in 1954 plans 'for the development of nuclear propulsion for large naval vessels'.

With nuclear-powered carriers, onboard reactors heat pressurized water and turn it into high-pressure steam. This high-pressure steam is then employed to power a ship's main propulsion turbine engines, which are mechanical, turbine generators, and auxiliary machinery. It also provides the steam required by the ship's catapults.

Unlike conventionally-powered carriers that must refuel every few thousand miles, nuclear-powered carriers have the ability to steam at high speed for up to a million miles. However, like conventionally-powered carriers, nuclear-powered carriers must still be replenished constantly with aviation fuel and ordnance for their aircraft plus food and other supplies for their crews.

As nuclear reactors produce a great deal of radiation, the areas of a ship in which they are located must be heavily shielded to protect the engineering crew. The level of training required among the engineering crew of nuclear-powered carriers is much higher than that of their conventionally-powered counterparts. Since nuclear reactors do not produce the exhaust gases of ships powered by fuel oil-fired boilers, nuclear-powered ships do not require stacks, which does free up a certain amount of room on a carrier's island.

The First Nuclear-Powered US Navy Carrier

In 1956 Congress authorized the construction of the first nuclear-powered carrier. On 4 February 1958, at the same time the keel of the new ship was being laid down, Secretary of the Navy William B. Franke announced that it would be assigned the proud name *Enterprise* to perpetuate the famous Second World War *Yorktown*-class carrier USS *Enterprise* (CV-6) and its five naval predecessors.

This first nuclear-powered carrier for the US navy was commissioned in November 1961 as the USS *Enterprise* (CVAN-65), with the letter 'N' within the letter suffix designation code representing the fact that it was nuclear-powered. It was originally envisioned that the USS *Enterprise* would be the lead in a class of six ships.

The first commander of the USS *Enterprise* was Captain (later Vice Admiral) Vincent de Poix. In early 1962 he described some of the abilities of his new ship:

> There are four rudders, one almost directly astern of each propeller. This provides excellent maneuverability at all speeds as well as tactical diameters in turns which compares with much smaller ships …
>
> Her ability to launch a strike on the enemy from one position, recover, and launch another 24 hours later from an unpredictable position more than 800 miles away from her previous strike position will constantly be a factor in causing the enemy to utilize protective forces that could be deployed elsewhere.
>
> If a show of force is required, *Enterprise* can be on distant station in a shorter period of time than any other ship in the fleet.

Ship Description

At the time it was built, the USS *Enterprise* was the largest ship ever constructed with a length of 1,123 feet and a full load displacement of 89,600 tons. The general shape and dimensions of the ship were based on the design of the *Kitty Hawk*-class carriers. The *Enterprise* typically carried 100 planes.

Like the previous *Kitty Hawk* class, the USS *Enterprise* had four steam-powered catapults and four deck-edge elevators. Its most distinctive external feature was the box-like design of the upper portion of its island, which had large flat-panel phased-array antennas mounted instead of the more conventional rotating radar antennas. The original radar design arrangement on the *Enterprise* was eventually removed and replaced by more conventional rotating radars.

During its many decades of service, the USS *Enterprise* went through a number of modernization programmes. In 1975 the US navy redesignated the letter suffix code for the ship from CVAN to CVN, when it received its own inventory of ASW aircraft.

Due to the cost of building the *Enterprise*, the US navy decided not to build any additional examples of the ship. It was inactivated in December 2012 because of the high cost of refuelling the eight nuclear reactors on board the ship. However, it will not be formally decommissioned until it is completely defuelled, which will take until 2015 or longer.

Nimitz-Class Carriers

Despite some early problems with the USS *Enterprise*, mainly centred on its phased-array radar system, the Secretary of Defense and Congress were generally very pleased with its operational performance. This resulted in Congress authorizing the construction of a new, more affordable class of nuclear-powered carriers, designated the *Nimitz* class. They would be based around the design of the *Kitty Hawk*-class carriers, which in turn had been based on the cancelled USS *United States* (CVA-58).

The first ship in the *Nimitz* class was the USS *Nimitz* (CVAN-68) that was laid down in June 1968 but not commissioned until May 1975. This long gestation period pushed back the planned commissioning date of the follow-on *Nimitz*-class carriers, resulting in a dramatic increase in their cost. President Jimmy Carter responded to this additional expense by boldly suggesting that the US navy cancel the *Nimitz* class and build a class of smaller and more affordable carriers. As might be expected, the majority of the US navy's senior leadership reacted very badly to the president's view on what was best for the service and with its Congressional supporters overcame his objections. Congress would go on to authorize funding for the construction of additional *Nimitz*-class carriers.

Some within the US navy and the preceding President Gerald Ford administration had also believed that smaller non-nuclear-powered carriers might be a solution to the high cost of nuclear-powered vessels and had done various studies on the matter beginning in the 1970s. However, none ever came to fruition. These proposed smaller, non-nuclear-powered carriers went by different names: Sea Control Ship (SCS), mid-size carrier (CVV) and the VSTOL Support Ship (VSS), the acronym 'VSTOL' standing for Vertical/Short Take-Off and Landing.

Additional *Nimitz*-Class Carriers Authorized

The USS *Nimitz* was followed by the USS *Dwight D. Eisenhower* (CVAN-69). In June 1975 both ships were reclassified with the letter suffix designation code CVN as they had their own dedicated ASW aircraft, making them multi-mission carriers.

The following eight *Nimitz*-class carriers were assigned the letter suffix designation code CVN from their commissioning date: USS *Carl Vinson* (CVN-70), USS *Theodore Roosevelt* (CVN-71), USS *Abraham Lincoln* (CVN-72), USS *George Washington* (CVN-73), USS *John C. Stennis* (CVN-74), USS *Harry S. Truman* (CVN-75), USS *Ronald Reagan* (CVN-76) and USS *George H.W. Bush* (CVN-77). The last was commissioned in January 2009, thirty-four years after the first in its class. All ten *Nimitz*-class carriers continue in service to this day and remain the tip of the spear in America's military projection around the globe.

Class Description

Nimitz-class carriers are twenty-four storeys high and require more than 900 miles of cable and wiring, 60,000 tons of structural steel and almost a million pounds of aluminium. The four bronze propellers that push them through the seas are 21 feet across and weigh 66,220 pounds each. There are nearly 30,000 light fixtures and

2,000 phones aboard a *Nimitz*-class carrier. A distillation plant produces 400,000 gallons of fresh water daily for each ship and its crew. That is enough for 2,000 suburban homes every day. The kitchens on board the ships prepare 18,150 meals per day.

The *Nimitz*-class carriers have an overall length of 1,094 feet with a full load displacement of almost 100,000 tons in the last units constructed. They can carry up to ninety planes in an emergency, with a typical number today being around fifty-six planes.

As with the previous *Kitty Hawk* class, the *Nimitz*-class carriers have four steam-powered catapults and four deck-edge elevators. Unlike the USS *Enterprise* (CVAN-65) that had eight A2W nuclear reactors, the *Nimitz*-class ships have only two of the latest-generation A4W nuclear reactors, the extra space being employed for many other purposes such as storage of aviation fuel and ordnance.

The Merits of Nuclear-Powered Carriers

The US navy preference for nuclear-powered carriers over their conventionally-powered equivalents was addressed in an August 1998 Government Accounting Office (GAO) report entitled 'U.S. Navy Aircraft Carriers: Cost Effectiveness of Conventionally and Nuclear-Powered Carriers'. The following extract partly summarizes the GAO's conclusions:

> Each type of carrier offers certain advantages. For example, conventionally powered carriers spend less time in maintenance, and as a result, they can provide more forward presence coverage. By the same token, nuclear carriers can store larger quantities of aviation fuel and munitions and, as a result, are less dependent on at-sea replenishment. There was little difference in the operational effectiveness of nuclear and conventional carriers in the Persian Gulf War …

Nimitz-Class Replacement Carrier

With the extremely long lead-in time between the authorization of a modern carrier and its commissioning, the US navy began thinking about the replacement for the *Nimitz*-class carriers as far back as the early 1990s. The first ship in this new proposed class of carriers would be a prototype referred to as the CVX.

In 1998 a US navy spokesman stated that the CVX prototype would be designed with a 'clean sheet of paper', suggesting that it would not be an evolutionary improvement over the previous *Nimitz*-class carriers but a revolutionary improvement with a dramatic rise in operational capabilities. Also implied was the fact that the CVX might not be nuclear-powered and would be more affordable and less costly to operate than the preceding *Nimitz* class.

Despite the 1998 pronouncement by the US navy on what they visualized for the CVX prototype, the funding necessary for the implementation of the revolutionary ship never materialized. Instead, in 2001 the new Secretary of Defense, Donald Rumsfeld, proposed that a prototype carrier be built as an evolutionary improvement over the previous *Nimitz*-class carriers and be labelled as CVX-1. It would be followed into production by the building of a more revolutionary improved *Nimitz*-class carrier designated the CVX-2.

The US navy then decided to merge the concept of the CVX-1 and CVX-2 into a single ship initially referred to as the CVN-21, with the numbers in the designation code representing the twenty-first century. Building of the new carrier, named the *Gerald R. Ford* and given the designation code CVN-78, began in 2007 with a tentative commissioning date of 2016. As indicated by the ship's letter suffix designation code, the *Gerald R. Ford* is nuclear-powered.

Carrier Description

The PCU (Pre-Commissioning Unit) *Gerald R. Ford* is 1,106 feet long and when commissioned it is estimated that it will have a full load displacement of over 100,000 tons. It will carry approximately seventy-five aircraft that will be launched by four catapults. Aircraft will be moved between the flight deck and hangar deck by three deck-edge elevators instead of the four on the previous *Nimitz*-class carriers.

The island on the *Gerald R. Ford* is smaller and located further aft than seen on the previous *Nimitz*-class carriers. To increase the number of missions (sorties) that the ship's aircraft can perform and at the same time reduce the number of personnel needed, a great deal of automation was incorporated into the carrier's final design.

From the Naval Sea System Command comes this passage describing the reasons why the new *Ford* class of carriers will be more cost-effective than the previous *Nimitz* class:

> Each ship in the new class will save more than $4 billion in total ownership costs during its 50-year service life, compared to the *Nimitz*-class. The CVN 78 is designed to operate effectively with nearly 700 fewer crew members than a CVN 68-class ship. Improvements in the ship design will allow the embarked air wing to operate with approximately 400 fewer personnel. New technologies and ship design features are expected to reduce watch standing and maintenance workload for the crew … The *Gerald R. Ford* class is designed to maximize the striking power of the embarked carrier air wing. The ship's systems and configuration are optimized to maximize the sortie generation rate (SGR) of attached strike aircraft, resulting in a 33 per cent increase in SGR over the *Nimitz* class. The ship's configuration and electrical generating plant are designed to accommodate new systems, including direct energy weapons, during its 50-year service life.

The *Gerald R. Ford* will be fitted with an Electromagnetic Aircraft Launch System (EMALS) when commissioned, in place of the steam-powered catapults currently employed on the *Nimitz*-class carriers. The advantages provided by installing the EMALS on the *Gerald R. Ford*, according to the US navy, are numerous. These include a reduction in size and weight, plus requiring less maintenance and therefore fewer personnel to operate. According to the programme manager for the EMALS, it will be able:

> to launch today's current air wing as well as all future carrier aircraft platforms in the U.S. Navy's inventory through 2030 with reduced wind-over-the-deck requirements when compared to steam catapults, and additional capability for aircraft growth during the 50-year life of a carrier.

To supplement the EMALS on the *Gerald R. Ford* it will also be fitted with the new Advanced Arresting Gear (AAG). This employs an electric motor-based system in place of the existing hydraulic arresting gear system. It has been stated by the US navy that the AAG will be much more reliable than the existing arresting gear system. It is planned to eventually upgrade the *Nimitz*-class carriers with the AAG.

The last two *Nimitz*-class carriers, the USS *Ronald Reagan* and USS *George H.W. Bush* were fitted with a new Advanced Recovery Control (ARC) system which is digitally controlled. This was in contrast to the previous Mk. 7 mechanically-controlled arresting gear system fitted to the first eight *Nimitz*-class carriers commissioned.

Two other carriers in what is now referred to as the *Gerald R. Ford* or *Ford* class have also been authorized: the *John F. Kennedy* (CVN-79) and the *Enterprise* (CVN-80). Construction on the *John F. Kennedy* began in 2011, with construction of the *Enterprise* scheduled to begin in 2018. Current plans call for eventually building seven more *Ford*-class carriers to replace the ten existing *Nimitz*-class carriers on a one-for-one basis. It is anticipated that the last *Nimitz*-class carrier will be decommissioned in 2058.

(*Above*) The US navy's second nuclear-powered ship – and the first nuclear-powered carrier – was the USS *Enterprise* (CVAN-65), seen here early in its service career. The USS *Enterprise* was launched in September 1960 and commissioned the following year. It was built at Newport News Shipbuilding, Virginia, as were all subsequent US navy nuclear-powered carriers. (*NNAM*)

(*Opposite page*) A close-up image of the original island design of the USS *Enterprise*, which differed from all the other US navy nuclear-powered carriers. The island's upper box-like form was dictated by the use of the billboard-shaped phased-array radar system developed by the Hughes Corporation and referred to as the SCANFAR system. The dome on top of the ship's island is covered with electronic warfare (EW) antennas. (*NNAM*)

(*Above*) Smoke is billowing from raging fires on the aft flight deck of the USS *Enterprise*, which occurred on 14 January 1969. The fire began when a Zuni rocket's warhead fitted on a parked F-4 Phantom II detonated. Swift action by the carrier's damage-control parties eventually brought the fire under control. However, 28 men died in the incident, another 334 were injured and 15 of the ship's aircraft were destroyed. (*NNAM*)

(*Opposite page*) The phased-array radar system originally fitted on the USS *Enterprise* proved unreliable in service. A decision was made to remove it and replace it with conventional rotating radar antennas. This change occurred during a refit that took place between 1979 and 1980 and is reflected in this picture of the ship's reconfigured island. Also visible in the same photograph is the ship's flight-deck anti-fire sprinkler system being tested. (*NNAM*)

(*Above*) The USS *Enterprise* was re-designated as a 'CVN' in 1975, reflecting its new role as a multi-purpose carrier rather than strictly an attack carrier. Pictured is the USS *Enterprise* in September 2012 during its last operational deployment which concluded on 4 November 2012 when it returned to its home port at Naval Station Norfolk, Virginia. (*DOD*)

(*Opposite page*) The USS *Nimitz* (CVAN-68), seen here, is the lead carrier in the nuclear-powered *Nimitz* class of ten. It was commissioned in May 1975 and at that time was the largest and most costly ship the US navy had ever taken into service. The ship's flight-deck configuration was very similar to that of the conventionally-powered *Forrestal*-class carriers that appeared in the 1950s, with four deck-edge elevators and four steam-powered catapults. (*DOD*)

(*Above*) The island design of the USS *Nimitz* and subsequent *Nimitz*-class carriers was similar in overall configuration to that of the conventionally-powered *Kitty Hawk*-class carriers, minus the stack. A feature adopted from the *Kitty Hawk* class that appeared on many of the *Nimitz*-class supercarriers was a large mast aft of the ship's island, as seen here, now surmounted by an air-search radar. (*DOD*)

(*Opposite above*) The Sikorsky SH-3H Sea King is seen here on the flight deck of a *Nimitz*-class carrier. The twin-engine helicopter first entered service with the US navy in 1961, with the last being pulled from service in 2006. The helicopter's main role when assigned to US navy carriers was ASW and it was equipped with dipping sonar, sono-buoys, magnetic anomaly detector, torpedoes, depth charges, a data link, chaff and a tactical navigation system. (*DOD*)

(*Opposite below*) The second ship commissioned in the *Nimitz* class of carriers was the USS *Dwight D. Eisenhower* (CVAN-69), seen here with its crew washing down and cleaning the flight deck. The uppermost windowed compartment projecting out over the flight deck from the forward portion of the ship's island is the Primary Flight Control (Pri-Fly). (*DOD*)

(*Left*) An interior view of the Pri-Fly of a *Nimitz*-class carrier with the air-operations officer, commonly referred to as the 'air boss', monitoring the launch and recovery of aircraft upon his ship. Air bosses and their seconds-in-command, the air officer assistants nicknamed the 'mini-boss', are responsible for all the air operations on their ship's flight deck as well as any of the carrier's aircraft flying within approximately 11 miles of their vessel. (*DOD*)

(*Opposite page*) Reporting to the air boss on *Nimitz*-class supercarriers is the aircraft-handling officer, commonly nicknamed the 'handler' or 'mangler', located in a compartment at the bottom of the ship's island. Within this compartment is a clear plastic table known as the aircraft 'spotting board' or 'ouija board' as seen in this picture. The flight deck and hangar deck are outlined on the spotting board. It is upon these tables that small cut-outs of aircraft are moved about to keep track of the location of the real planes on the ship. (*DOD*)

(*Below*) The hangar decks on *Nimitz*-class carriers are 30 feet tall, 850 feet in length and 140 feet in width. They are narrower than the carriers' flight decks, located three levels above them, as they do not extend into the overhanging sponsons that support the wider flight decks. The overhanging sponson spaces beneath the flight deck of a *Nimitz*-class carrier are made up of numerous compartments hosting a variety of functions. (*DOD*)

(*Above*) As well as the four very large deck-edge elevators on *Nimitz*-class carriers, there are also four much smaller weapon elevators, one of which is seen here. They are employed to transport a variety of objects, including bombs and missiles, from the magazine-handling spaces located far below the ship's hangar deck to the flight deck. (*DOD*)

(*Opposite above*) Located above the hangar deck of *Nimitz*-class carriers and directly below the armoured flight deck is the gallery deck. Squadron ready rooms where pilots are briefed prior to their missions as seen in this picture are located on the gallery deck of *Nimitz*-class carriers. There may be as many as eight squadrons assigned to a carrier air wing based on a *Nimitz*-class carrier. (*DOD*)

(*Opposite below*) The aircraft on *Nimitz*-class carriers are moved between flight deck and hangar deck by four massive 3,880-sq.ft deck-edge elevators that can hoist up to 130,000lb each. In the foreground of this picture of a *Nimitz*-class carrier elevator is a Lockheed S-3 Viking multi-mission aircraft. Behind it is a McDonnell Douglas F/A-18 Hornet strike-fighter. (*DOD*)

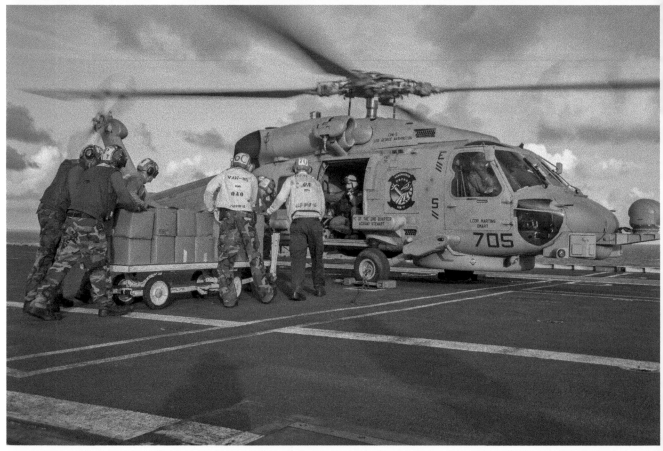

(*Above*) It is on the flight deck where the aircraft of the *Nimitz*-class carriers are fuelled prior to being launched, as seen in this photograph. The *Nimitz*-class carriers have storage space for approximately 4 million gallons of JP-5 aviation fuel, nicknamed 'motion lotion'. The *Nimitz*-class vessels can store 50 per cent more aviation fuel than older-generation conventionally-powered carriers because they don't need to dedicate large amounts of bunkerage to storing fuel for propulsion. (*DOD*)

(*Opposite above*) The aircraft elevators on the *Nimitz*-class supercarriers are also employed to bring up large amounts of ordnance from the ships' hangar decks to their flight decks, as seen in this photograph taken in 2003 during Operation IRAQI FREEDOM. On the elevator appear Guided Bomb Units (GBU) which are guided to their intended targets by a combination of an inertial navigation system and Global Positioning System (GPS). (*DOD*)

(*Opposite below*) The replacement for the Sikorsky SH-3H Sea King on *Nimitz*-class carriers was the Sikorsky SH-60 Seahawk. Later upgrades resulted in the MH-60R version shown here. The twin-engine helicopter can perform a wide variety of roles including that of a gunship. In that capacity it can be armed with both machine guns and anti-tank missiles. It is aided in that role and others by a forward-looking infrared (FLIR) sensor, seen here mounted on the front of the helicopter. (*DOD*)

Once the aircraft on a *Nimitz*-class carrier flight deck are fuelled and armed they will be directed to one of the ship's four catapults by a plane director, who is under the overall supervision of the air boss. When the plane is lined up with a catapult, nicknamed the 'cat track', a young crewman wearing a green jersey with a green helmet will attach a launch (tow) bar from the front wheel assembly of an aircraft into the shuttle of the catapult launch system, as shown here. (*DOD*)

Upon an aircraft being secured to the catapult launch system on board a *Nimitz*-class carrier, a catapult crewman holds up a number board with the plane's expected take-off weight that they will show to both the pilot and the catapult officer, nicknamed the 'cat officer' or 'shooter'. During the Second World War the catapult officer was referred to as the flight-deck dispatcher. (*DOD*)

The four football-field-length steam catapults on the *Nimitz*-class supercarriers are numbered one to four, with the starboard-side bow catapult track, seen here on the USS *Carl Vinson* (CVN-70), labelled number one. The port-side bow catapult track visible is designated number two. The innermost catapult on the port-side angled deck section is number three and the outermost is number four. *(DOD)*

If both the pilot of an aircraft about to be launched from a *Nimitz*-class carrier and the catapult officer agree on the aircraft's weight, using hand signals the catapult officer will launch the plane with a powerful jet of pressurized steam. The catapult officers on current *Nimitz*-class carriers are located in one of two retractable armoured compartments as seen here, referred to as the Integrated Catapult Control Station (ICCS) and nicknamed 'the bubble'. *(DOD)*

As an aircraft aboard a *Nimitz*-class carrier is guided to its launching catapult, a large moveable portion of the flight deck referred to as the Jet Blast Deflector (JBD) is raised behind it at an angle of 50 degrees, as seen in this picture. As can be expected from its designation, the job of the JBD is to deflect the massive blast of hot gasses generated by jet aircraft as they throttle up their engines prior to being launched from the flight deck. *(DOD)*

When an aircraft is successfully launched from a *Nimitz*-class carrier, the responsibility for that plane passes from the air boss and mini-boss to a departure controller in the Carrier Air Traffic Control Center (CATCC), as shown here. Upon returning to their ship, pilots will once again be in touch with the CATCC via approach controllers as they get closer to the ship. When within 11 miles of their carrier, the air boss and the CATCC work together to safely return the incoming aircraft to the ship's flight deck. *(DOD)*

Since 2004 all *Nimitz*-class carriers have been fitted with the Improved Fresnel Lens Optical Landing System (IFLOLS) shown here. Rather than using incandescent bulbs as did the FLOLS, the IFLOLS employs a fibre-optic 'source' light projected through the various coloured lenses of the device, which produces a brighter and sharper light that pilots can see at greater distances than the older-generation FLOLS. *(DOD)*

(*Left*) Despite the many technological improvements that have come into service on board *Nimitz*-class carriers to assist pilots into returning to their ships, LSOs as seen here continue to play an important role in that operation. The device being held in the upright arms of the LSO is referred to as the 'pickle' and when a button is pushed on the device, it will warn the pilot off his approach by means of red warning lights. (*DOD*)

(*Opposite page*) When landing on the flight deck of a *Nimitz*-class carrier it is the pilot's job to catch one of four cross-deck pendants, commonly called arresting wires, with a metal bar referred to as a 'tail hook' seen in this photograph, which drops from the rear of the aircraft's fuselage. If the pilot fails to catch any of the arresting wires they will perform what is known as a 'bolter' and be forced to go around for another attempt. (*DOD*)

(*Below*) Being lowered into a space just below the flight deck of a *Nimitz*-class carrier undergoing refitting at a shipyard is an arrestor-gear engine. The weight of a returning aircraft is very important to the arrestor-gear personnel so that they can apply the correct amount of tension in the arrestor-gear engine. If too much tension is set, it could cause structural damage to a plane. Too little tension and the aircraft could end up going over the ship's bow. (*DOD*)

(*Above*) Constant practice hones the skills of the crash and salvage crews serving on board all the *Nimitz*-class carriers. They are seen here using a McDonnell Douglas F/A-18 Hornet during a training session. The twin-engine multimission aircraft first entered US navy and US Marine Corps service in 1983 as the replacement for earlier-generation aircraft. (*DOD*)

(*Opposite above*) Found on the island of every *Nimitz*-class carrier is the Pilot Landing Aid Television (PLAT) system. It is located in a small, windowed compartment as seen here at the forward portion of the island directly below the flag bridge. The sailor assigned to the PLAT system films the recovery of the ship's aircraft for later review by a pilot's superiors to determine their level of proficiency. (*DOD*)

(*Opposite below*) During launch and recovery operations on board *Nimitz*-class carriers there is always a crew manning a P-16 fire-fighting vehicle, as shown here. The P-16 stores a foam extinguishing agent that is projected from the nozzle at the front of the vehicle. Two crew members of the P-16 shown are wearing what are referred to as fire-proximity suits. (*DOD*)

(*Above*) The USS *Enterprise* (CVAN-65) was originally intended to have been fitted with the RIM-2 Terrier surface-to-air missile (SAM) system but they were never fitted in order to keep the ship's cost down. Eventually the ship was fitted with the RIM-7 Seasparrow SAM system. Constantly under improvement, the current version shown here at the moment of launching is referred to as the NATO Seasparrow Surface Missile System (NSSMS Mark 57). (*DOD*)

(*Opposite above*) To assist in moving damaged aircraft around the flight deck of *Nimitz*-class carriers there is a single large crash and salvage crane truck, as seen here. The crane truck is always nicknamed the 'Tilly'. Such is the importance of these machines that no flight operations can be conducted on a *Nimitz*-class carrier without an operational Tilly. (*DOD*)

(*Opposite below*) The job of fighting fires on US navy ships is considered an all-hands responsibility and is constantly practised, as seen in this picture on a *Nimitz*-class carrier of an emergency damage-control team. All the personnel shown in this photograph are wearing oxygen breathing apparatus (OBA). Behind the nozzle-man is the scene leader holding a thermal camera to aid in identifying the source of a fire aboard the ship. (*DOD*)

(*Right*) The earliest version of the RIM-7 Seasparrow SAM system, mounted on the USS *Enterprise* in August 1966 and on follow-on nuclear-powered carriers, was manually aimed by the Mark 115 radar director seen here fitted with two circular drums. One of the drums contained the antenna for the illumination radar that painted incoming threats. The other drum held a flat-plate planar-array antenna to detect the reflected radiation coming off a target which a missile would then be directed to. (*DOD*)

(*Below*) A starboard-side view of the island on the USS *Nimitz* (CVAN-68). Visible on two open balconies at the very top level of the ship's island are the twin circular heads of the fully-automated SPS-65 low-altitude illumination and acquisition radar antennas that make up the Mark 91 Fire Control System. It was this system that replaced the manually-operated Mark 115 radar director in the control of the original RIM-7 Seasparrow SAM system. (*DOD*)

Supplementing the RIM-7 Seasparrow SAM system on the USS *Enterprise* (CVAN-65), the conventionally-powered *Kitty Hawk*-class carriers and the follow-on *Nimitz* class was the Mark 15 Phalanx Close-In Weapon System (CIWS) seen here. It is a radar-guided 20mm gun system capable of firing 3,000–4,500 rounds per minute and intended to defeat any close-range incoming aerial threats. *(DOD)*

As with all the air-defence systems on US navy carriers, the Mark 15 Phalanx CIWS has been constantly improved. Pictured is the latest version, referred to as the Phalanx Block 1B. It features a forward-looking infrared sensor seen here mounted on the right side of the weapon's radome. *(DOD)*

(*Above*) A new addition to the close-range defensive screen of *Nimitz*-class carriers is the RIM-116 Rolling Airframe Missile (RAM), seen here at the moment of firing. The RIM-116 RAM is primarily intended to engage anti-ship cruise missiles. Unlike the NATO Seasparrow Surface Missile System, the RIM-116 RAM is a fire-and-forget missile system. The launcher system itself contains twenty-one missiles. (*DOD*)

(*Opposite above*) An extremely close-in defensive weapon fitted on *Nimitz*-class carriers is the air-cooled .50 calibre (12.7mm) M2 Browning machine gun seen here. It is not intended to deal with fast-moving aerial threats to the ship. Rather, when in confined waters or foreign ports it is intended to protect the carrier from such threats as small suicide boats filled with explosives. (*DOD*)

(*Opposite below*) Many critics have long contended that the *Nimitz*-class carriers are much more vulnerable than the US navy has ever admitted. To answer those critics and to prove to those who fund the carriers of the survivability of the ships, a number of tests have been conducted. An unclassified test occurred in 1987 when the stationary USS *Theodore Roosevelt* (CVN-71) was subjected to a large underwater explosion to confirm the structural durability of the ship's design. (*DOD*)

(*Above*) The USS *Abraham Lincoln* (CVN-72), shown here, was the fifth ship commissioned in the *Nimitz* class of carriers. In April 1993 it was the first US navy carrier to host female aviators; a novelty back then but now considered a normal fact of life aboard all *Nimitz*-class ships. The vessel played an important role in Operation IRAQI FREEDOM in 2003, with its pilots and air-crews dropping over a million pounds of ordnance on Iraqi military targets during the conflict. (*DOD*)

(*Opposite above*) The USS *Ronald Reagan* (CVN-76), seen here in profile, has an island of a somewhat different design from the five *Nimitz*-class carriers commissioned into service before it. The most noticeable external change is the removal of the large main mast aft of the ship's island on the flight deck surmounted by an air-search radar antenna. The air-search radar is now mounted on a much shorter stub main mast located on the roof of the rear portion of the carrier's island. (*DOD*)

(*Opposite below*) From the bottom of a dry dock looking up is a photograph of the stern of the USS *John C. Stennis* (CVN-74) having one of its massive propellers replaced. The two nuclear reactors and associated machinery that power the *Nimitz*-class carriers are located in the bottom of their hulls. They are protected by a double hull that can absorb and dissipate the energy generated by conventional mines or torpedoes. (*DOD*)

(*Above*) Pictured prior to commissioning is the USS *Harry S. Truman* (CVN-75). As with all *Nimitz*-class carriers, the ship's flight deck is approximately 4.5 acres. The armoured flight deck is covered by a non-skid surface. As can be imagined, the price of building such massive ships is high. Minus the aircraft of an assigned carrier wing, the last *Nimitz*-class carrier cost $6 billion. (*DOD*)

(*Above*) Looking rearward from the bow of the USS *Ronald Reagan* can be seen the island of the ship. The white domes on the island are the radomes for the ship's many satellite communication antennas, which fall under the heading of satellite communications (SATCOM) in the US navy's lexicon. That part of the second-level navigation bridge extending out over the starboard side of the island is employed by the command staff when the ship is being replenished at sea or docking. (*DOD*)

(*Opposite below*) The USS *Ronald Reagan* (CVN-76) is seen here during a test to check its material condition and battle-readiness. The angle at which this *Nimitz*-class carrier is leaning and the wake being generated by the ship as it ploughs through the water are indicators of the speed that these carriers can achieve. The US navy keeps the top speed of their *Nimitz*-class carriers a secret but will state that it is 30 knots (35 mph) and above. (*DOD*)

(*Above*) A massive lift is shown lowering a 700-ton uncompleted island onto the starboard flight deck of the USS *George H.W. Bush* (CVN-77) at the Northrop Grumman Newport News Shipyard in Virginia. As with the USS *George Washington* (CVN-73), there is no separate main mast aft of the island on the flight deck. Instead, a stub main mast projects from the roof of the rear portion of the carrier's uncompleted island. (*DOD*)

(*Opposite above*) The upper bow of the unfinished USS *George H.W. Bush* is being brought together with the rest of the ship's hull at the Northrop Grumman Newport News Shipyard in March 2002. The ship was commissioned in January 2009 and was operationally deployed the following year. New features on the vessel included a lighter non-skid flight-deck covering material that shaved 100 tons from the ship's weight. (*DOD*)

(*Opposite below*) Shown launching from a *Nimitz*-class carrier is a Boeing F/A-18F Super Hornet multi-mission aircraft. It is a 20 per cent larger evolutionary improvement of the McDonnell Douglas F/A-18 Hornet, now referred to as the 'Legacy Hornet'. Boeing acquired McDonnell Douglas in August 1997. The Boeing F/A-18F Super Hornet entered US navy service in 1999 and is nicknamed the 'Rhino'. (*DOD*)

(*Above*) Pictured still in dry dock during its launching ceremony is the unfinished USS *Gerald R. Ford* (CVN-78). It is the first ship in the brand-new *Gerald R. Ford* class of supercarriers. It has a new bulbous lower bow section seen here that improves hull efficiency by adding buoyancy to the forward end of the ship. Total cost of the ship when completed is expected to be $14 billion. (*DOD*)

(*Opposite above*) The second ship in the new *Ford* class of carriers will be the USS *John F. Kennedy* (CVN-79), seen here in model form. Construction of the vessel began in February 2011 and it is expected to be completed by 2020. The island on the *Ford* class of supercarriers will have only a single large foremast projecting out of the roof rather than the two separate masts seen on *Nimitz*-class carriers. (*DOD*)

(*Opposite below*) The intended replacement for the 'legacy' McDonnell Douglas F/A-18 Hornet, and to complement the Boeing F/A-18 Super Hornet on the *Nimitz* and *Ford* class of carriers, is the Lockheed Martin F-35C multi-mission aircraft seen here. The single-engine, single-seat F-35C is a variant of the standard F-35, originally known as the Joint Strike Fighter (JSF), and has stealth features. It first entered service with the US navy in 2013 and may represent the last generation of manned carrier aircraft employed by the service. (*DOD*)

On the horizon for use on the *Nimitz* and *Ford* class of carriers are unmanned combat aerial vehicles, the possible future of carrier aviation. Pictured on the flight deck of a *Nimitz*-class carrier is a tailless Northrop Grumman demonstration drone, designated the X-47B. It was successfully launched and recovered from *Nimitz*-class supercarriers in 2013. It has a wing span of 62 feet and two weapon bays, plus stealth features. *(DOD)*

Notes

Notes

Notes

Notes

Notes

Notes

Notes

Notes